GENEROSITY
VIRTUE IN CIVIL SOCIETY

GENEROSITY
VIRTUE IN CIVIL SOCIETY

TIBOR R. MACHAN

CATO
INSTITUTE
Washington, D.C.

Library of Congress Cataloging-in-Publication Data

Machan, Tibor R.
    Generosity : virtue in civil society / by Tibor R. Machan.
        p.   cm.
    Includes bibliographical references and index.
    ISBN 1-882577-53-1. — ISBN 1-882577-54-X (pbk.)
    1. Generosity.   2. Generosity—Political aspects.   3. Welfare state—
Moral and ethical aspects.   I. Title.
BJ1533.G4M33   1998
179'.9—dc21   97-51252
                                                                            CIP

CATO INSTITUTE
1000 Massachusetts Ave., N.W.
Washington, D.C. 20001

To my daughter Erin

Contents

Preface

Generosity is a moral virtue that cannot flourish in a welfare state or in any sort of command economy, because to be generous is to *voluntarily* help others in certain ways. It will, however, flourish in a free society. That is what this monograph will argue and demonstrate.

Generous acts require the right to private property. The point is ancient—Aristotle argued it nearly 2,500 years ago. But its full import has never been widely enough appreciated. Indeed, many who proselytize for generosity, compassion, kindness, and charity have resisted the establishment of the right to private property as a firm principle of law. For example, the philosopher Thomas Nagel criticized free society as an actual hindrance to generous conduct. As he put it,

> Most people are not generous when asked to give voluntarily, and it is unreasonable to ask that they should be. Admittedly there are cases in which a person should do something although it would not be right to force him to do it. But here I believe that the reverse is true. Sometimes it is proper to force people to do something even though it is not true that they should do it without being forced. It is acceptable to compel people to contribute to the support of the indigent by automatic taxation, but unreasonable to insist that in the absence of such a system they ought to contribute voluntarily.[1]

That position is the opposite of the present author's. We shall have occasion to examine it in detail in due course. For now, it needs to be noted that such a view is exceedingly pessimistic and ultimately self-defeating, for what one cannot require of free men and women morally will be impossible to demand of them politically. The system Nagel proposes only provides an excuse for people not to act generously, since their government does—or, more precisely, pretends to do—so for them.

Such an outlook injects into political life a spirit not of bona fide generosity but of subterfuge, encouraging moral lethargy and shattered hopes and expectations. One reason the welfare state is often a kind of Hobbesian war of all (special-interest groups) against all is that the ultimately cynical view of human nature Nagel spells out constitutes a good part of the foundation of the welfare state.

The welfare state unabashedly perverts the idea of the right to private property and thus stands as a substantial obstacle to at least one form of human moral intercourse: kindness and generosity among the citizenry. That system has placed its confidence, instead, in forced "charity," wealth redistribution at the point of a gun, which does not by any means encourage goodwill among us. It fosters resentment, bureaucratic inefficiency, and frustration—but most of all, it blocks the only way moral excellence can flourish, by way of free choice.

One's prime purpose in life is to be as happy as he can be. Happiness, or as the ancient Greeks who founded the Western moral tradition put it, *eudaimonia,* is success as the individual human being one has the potential to be. That is the broadest common moral purpose we share, although the details make all the difference in how we actually live our particular lives. In other words, the moral life of one person can be very, very different from the moral life of another, so the practice of any of the moral virtues can and does manifest itself in unique ways, depending on who one is. Yet there are basic common—albeit very general—features that such a life will exhibit, including the practice of the virtue of generosity.

Generosity, as the Greeks saw, is not tantamount to altruism, which means putting others first. To be generous means to extend goodwill toward others because one's own happiness is thereby enhanced, because one lives a fully human life if, among other things, one lives generously.

Politically, the right to be free—including the right to treat one another generously, stingily, kindly, callously, and so forth—is of primary importance for everyone. To make the right choices, human beings have to have their sovereignty as moral agents fully respected. That is the only way a creature of free will can be free to choose to act virtuously, including generously, and thus be capable of living a morally significant life.

Why, however, if one ought to strive to be a happy individual and ought to have one's right to liberty respected, should one also be generous, even charitable? Does that not imply that one ought to support a welfare state rather than the libertarian polity? Many prominent thinkers deny that—among them Milton Friedman, Charles Murray, Antony Flew, and a host of other economists, political scientists, and philosophers.

Others take the opposite view. James P. Sterba, who advocates the welfare state, believes that the free society in the classical-liberal or libertarian tradition fails to help the poor and so requires rethinking and upgrading to include welfare rights. Communitarians such as Charles Taylor, Amitai Etzioni, Robert Bellah and his colleagues, and Michael J. Sandel[2] think classical liberals and libertarians are mistaken about human nature, which leads them to forget about the necessary communal features of the best society. Those features require placing the right to liberty alongside other, more positive rights—for example, rights to safety and education—that the government must secure for all of us. Those features can even require us to give up the right to liberty itself as fictional. Sandel has recently lamented the loss of what he calls the republican virtues. Those amount to no less than a convivial submergence of oneself into the community, stressing social obligations instead of individual rights.

Those thinkers believe that, in their communities, men and women can be either completely free (i.e., uncoerced), and thus insufficiently decent toward each other, or at least mildly regimented, and thus made to behave properly. In short, we face here once again the well-known alleged opposition of freedom and virtue.

The critics are, however, wrong. No good reason for giving up on free men and women exists; there is only misguided fear, certainly as far as the virtue of generosity is concerned. Free men and women may not choose to use their limited resources for what someone else thinks is worthy of joint attention, even though it may be. But there are likely to be more than enough appeals to generosity in a free community to inspire each individual without the imposition of coercively forced obligations. Unless one has been so deluded as to strive for a utopian world of guaranteed perfect human conduct, one should trust women and men to be decent, including generous and charitable, without any "official" regimentation. They will then be free to build and sustain human communities that exhibit care, compassion, and kindness alongside prudence, industry, courage, and other virtues, without sacrificing personal sovereignty in the least.

First I will lay out the general case for connecting generosity with political liberty. I will then indicate how that case can influence our thinking about certain matters welfare statists think should lead one to abandon political and economic liberty. I will conclude this examination with a treatment of a particular problem: can the moral habit of donation—of blood, organs, emergency provisions—be coercively encouraged?

I want to thank Jim Chesher, Doug Rasmussen, Tom Palmer, Bill Davis, and Douglas J. Den Uyl for their support and help. I have learned much from Eric Mack, David Kelley, James Wallace, and Lester H. Hunt. I also thank the *Journal of Applied Philosophy* for permission to use some material that has appeared there, as well as the Earhart Foundation for supporting my earlier scholarly work on generosity. Kelly Russell Simpson's editorial work on the project is also much appreciated. My colleagues in the Auburn University Department of Philosophy, in particular Clifton Perry and Kelly Dean Jolley, have left their mark on this work with their customary generous criticism and suggestions for improvement.

1. Generosity, a Benevolent Virtue

Ordinary Generosity

Generous persons were originally understood to be ones whose basic nature was sound. Later the meaning of the term "generous" evolved and came to mean, roughly, a disposition or inclination to act benevolently toward some other persons. Still, the original meaning left its imprint.

We tend to take it that generous people are benevolent because of their character, not as a matter of deliberation or calculation. As a character trait, generosity inclines one to do good for others. It can manifest itself in small or large measures: "As he began to shave, he thought to turn off the running water in his hotel bathroom since the pressure during morning hours nearly vanished. If he restricted the flow somewhat in his sink, the rest of the guests would have a better chance at getting water to come out of their faucets." "When she heard that those folks wanted to get themselves on their feet, following their narrow escape from their wretched homeland, she went to her desk and wrote out and sent them a sizable check."

No direct personal gain is involved in generous conduct. A generous person doesn't think, "If I am good to them, I'll get this or that for my trouble." Generosity, when viewed under a microscope, is a member of the family of benevolent moral principles. One may be "benevolent" in a variety of ways, among them by being generous, charitable, kind, compassionate, or thoughtful. But what distinguishes generosity from, for example, kindness or compassion is not always clear. The terms are often used interchangeably, although kindness is more of an attitude, and an attitude need not issue in action. Compassion tends to presuppose the beneficiary is pitiable, heartbreaking, deserving of special care. When we are urged to be compassionate, it is toward those who are in trouble.

Generosity involves spontaneously doing good things—giving gifts, providing help or advice, showing tolerance or special consideration—for others, who may or may not be in trouble. The acts are spontaneous in that they flow from one's character, not from calculation or even deliberation. Character, in turn, is a gradually evolved collection of traits that we acquire through our rearing and, later, through perseverance, commitment, and resistance to laxness—all sustained through a kind of low-key reflection on how or who we ought to be.

Charity, in contrast, is benevolence arising from a sense of duty. One would be charitable by extending oneself toward others as a result of the realization that one has the duty to do something for them. A duty is an action that is morally prescribed, a matter of a rule or law that one must explicitly know before one can follow it. Generosity is more of a morally commendable trait, leading as it does to spontaneous acts. Those distinctions are not always observed in ordinary reflection and usage, but there are examples of our use of the terms that clearly suggest what is noted above.

When one talks of a generous person, one usually has in mind someone who does good for others as a matter of course, without hesitation. There is nothing forced or self-disciplined about it. One is not resisting greed when one is being generous. Charity, in contrast, involves telling oneself to give others what one ought to give them, because one has the explicit belief that one ought to give to them. Charity is deliberative, not spontaneous.

One might object that generosity flows from the discipline one has once exercised, just as good, smooth driving follows early training that was rigorous and required considerable direct mental focus. That is a good point, but it characterizes the way someone might *become* generous, not generosity itself. It misses an important aspect of generosity by ascribing to a given action a quality that has not yet been absorbed within the agent. Generosity, in contrast, is such a quality—absorbed and ready to go into action effortlessly, as it were, on all appropriate occasions. Charitable conduct may involve deliberate discipline or concentration, but generosity does not. It is a character trait, an aspect of a person and not a form of behavior a person imposes on himself.

Yet one's generosity is extended as a result of a generalized— perhaps even automatized or self-programmed—outlook or disposition one has toward (some) other people in one's life. Generosity involves giving of oneself or what one has to those one finds precious or to persons or causes one thinks highly of or feels close to. Generosity flows from a generalized valuation of some other people or their goals.

Lack of generosity is a moral vice. That vice must, as must all moral vices, in principle be possible for the opposite, the moral virtue, to amount to something morally praiseworthy. Those who want to prohibit all vices—say, by transforming law enforcement agencies into a kind of massive vice squad—fail to appreciate that if vice is banned, unambiguous virtue becomes impossible: there will be no possibility of crediting people for making right choices.

In any case, *generosity is not self-sacrificial* in the way charity and even compassion can be. Nor is it calculating: there is no quid pro quo involved in generous acts. They involve giving without the expectation of anything like a return of favors. Of course, the virtue of generosity does involve a type of benefiting oneself, but only in the broadest possible sense. As David Schmidtz observes, "There are reasons to embrace and nurture our concern for others, reasons that have to do with what is conducive to our own health, survival, and growth."[1]

That self-benefiting comes from one's being a morally good person. In other words, being morally good is to one's benefit. That follows if moral virtues serve a person's project of living a good human life. Some moral theorists see no benefit to a person from that kind of life. But others do, and they have the best of the debate— what else could a good human life amount to than one that is good for the agent in a most fundamental respect? A good human life is the one thing valuable in and of itself, without reference to any other end or goal. But I will discuss that more extensively shortly.

To explore further the matter of the spontaneous element of generosity, we should consider that a generous person is not fighting to restrain some stingy inclination, needing to withstand the temptation of avarice. One is not generous for having restrained oneself from spending too much of one's money on a shopping spree and disciplined oneself to send care packages to starving Sudanese children. Rather, a generous person is acting, as it were, from second nature. Generous conduct is for such a person a matter of course. Generous people do not perform select good deeds or resist doing specific bad deeds. Rather, routinely in the course of their lives, they are giving, considerate, and expansive.

Generosity (as a moral virtue) would, then, be a benevolent trait that, although cultivated for oneself, would have become an unselfconscious way of conducting one's life. Under appropriate circumstances and without much effort, conduct helpful (but not by right

3

due) to others would flow from generous persons. When one is generous, one does not do for others what is due them by right. Positive-rights theorists might argue the contrary, but they are mistaken: Obligatory giving requires too much distributional calculation or, alternatively, rote conduct to amount to generosity. If my help is due someone—as it is, for example, my children—I am not being generous in giving it. If people are due respect for their human dignity—so that I ought not to intrude on their "moral space"— that again is not a matter of generosity. Such behavior involves knowing and acting on one's obligations toward others.

Yet it is not inappropriate to speak of a generous person as acting responsibly. The responsibility being referred to, however, would be in the sense of "carrying on appropriately in life," not "fulfillment of obligations." At one level, no one has the responsibility or obligation to be generous to anyone; at another, everyone may have the responsibility to cultivate the trait of generosity. Recall that we are concerned with generosity as a moral virtue and not merely as a rote habit that has been *acquired* (as distinct from being practiced) unselfconsciously; generosity must be self-cultivated.[2] Such an inclination can still be considered a virtue when one is predisposed to be generous by upbringing or perhaps even by temperament and then does not extinguish that predisposition, thus infusing it with some measure of free choice.[3] Ordinarily, however, without such an upbringing—one that inculcates in us an inclination we may simply build upon once it is cultivated—generosity is a self-cultivated inclination to act for the benefit of certain others.

Without the element of cultivation, a virtue could not be regarded as something morally good. The inclination to be helpful—to be benevolent—has to have been cultivated on one's own initiative and not have come about accidentally, perhaps as simply a family trait or a custom of one's community one picked up (and might not have picked up had one been brought up in another culture). Without that, it could not have moral significance—just as being a cute baby or a tall individual (thus photogenic or a candidate for basketball stardom, respectively) has no moral significance.

Yet "inclination" is the operative term here. Mature generosity does not manifest itself as a matter of deliberate choice. That may be appreciated by contrasting generosity with other candidates for moral virtues. For example, Christian love, or Christian charity—

4

agape or *caritas*—or some other religiously motivated love, which would spring from certain convictions as to what one's duties are, can issue in behavior similar to that of a generous person. But only if it becomes a generalized attitude prompting one to do good for others, without strain or discipline, will it qualify as generosity. Furthermore, such love is far less discriminating than generosity; that is to say, loving as conceived within the common understanding of Christian love is unconditional.

> Charity suffereth long, and is kind; charity envieth not; charity vaunteth not itself, is not puffed up,
> Doth not behave itself unseemly, seeketh not her own, is not easily provoked, thinketh no evil;
> Rejoiceth not in iniquity, but rejoiceth in the truth;
> Beareth all things, believeth all things, hopeth all things, endureth all things.
> Charity never faileth. . . . (1 Corinthians 13:4–8)

That kind of love might even be considered indiscriminate. Thus, in Christianity the commandment to love all as one loves oneself is taken to mean that one owes everyone a certain type of love—for example, charity if they are in need. It is irrelevant whether they have earned it, whether they have behaved themselves properly so that they deserve it, or, most important, whether one is personally inclined to extend oneself toward the beloved.

There is a debate about this: Some think that the purest form of Christian love might very well be the kind that is extended toward persons one finds offensive or repulsive. They argue that Jesus seems to have loved sinners the most. Others hold that the love of Christian charity is actually a call for respecting everyone's autonomy as a moral agent and does not require any kind of deference toward the sinful. Nor, they believe, does it demand self-sacrifice. Rather, it induces respect for individual rights. Augustine is at times taken to have given the latter interpretation to the love associated with Christian charity.[4]

In contrast, generosity, perhaps more than other traits and dispositions with possible moral ramifications, comes close to retaining the sort of status that all the virtues possess.[5] They are part of one's personality, deeply ingrained character traits. Generous, honest, temperate, or courageous conduct occurs as a matter of course, as a normal, natural feature of the life of a good human being. As

Lester Hunt suggests, generous conduct is akin to industriousness in that both are a part of character. "It is a sort of action which, in a relevant way, is not done for a reason at all."[6] Generous conduct is not deliberately chosen.

It is crucial to make a distinction between mere intentional and deliberate conduct. Of course, all deliberate conduct is intentional, but not all intentional conduct is deliberate. Mere intentional conduct can become virtually automatic, provided one has habituated oneself and thus knows what one is doing, whereas the latter is monitored, supervised as it is being done, checked out for its qualities. Both types of thoughtful conduct can be rational, but the type of rationality in intentional conduct need not involve deliberation: intentional conduct does involve assessing the situation, taking in information and invoking beliefs, but none of that is done at the time in a self-conscious, regimented fashion. Rather, the rationality is based on good habits of thought. In driving a car, one can notice the difference—experienced drivers do it intentionally but rarely deliberately, whereas novices do it all deliberately, with extensive self-supervision.

Generosity Is Not a Duty

It is important that a generous person is not doing good deeds for others because of a sense of duty or obligation. For some this may call into question whether generosity has moral significance. Morality is often construed exclusively in terms of duties, especially duties toward other persons. Charitable people make certain that they give to at least some of those who are in need.[7] And fair people act from duty to make sure that all get the same from goods they may have to distribute.

Consider some examples of where fairness is considered important: how teachers treat their students in class, or how a referee keeps score in a game or tells whether players of some team sport have adhered to the rules. In such circumstances fairness is expected as part of the job. Fairness in these cases is a duty, what one is obligated to do. When fairness is treated as a broad, basic moral virtue or principle, it is required that we be fair to all—indeed, we would be penalized for failing to be. If, as John Rawls claims, justice is fairness, and justice is something one must practice to avoid punishment, then fairness is different from what generosity commonly involves. In this way, fairness is an administrative virtue, whereas the basic moral virtues are constitutive of living itself.

The virtue of generosity—when generosity is a moral virtue rather than an accidental trait or inclination (which can then easily misfire, for example, through extending spontaneous benevolence toward undeserving persons)—does not belong within a morality concerned exclusively with rules. Such a conception of morality implies that one must always *deliberate* about what morality requires. One's actions would then be morally significant only if one purged oneself of inclinations (even an inclination to do the right thing).

Such an idea of morality does not leave room for the normal conception of the moral virtue of generosity—for example, as we think of a generous uncle or friend or neighbor. When, upon seeing that a person has fallen, another simply bends down to help, such an act does not flow from a sense of duty, from having figured out on the spot that this is what one now ought to do. Rather, it arises from a good nature, as it were, a readiness, upon finding the appropriate occasion, to extend oneself. It is to be generous, kind, helpful.

Generosity as a Moral Virtue

For now I will assume that moral virtues can exist; that is, human life includes moral virtues as voluntarily chosen or cultivated traits that guide the acting agent toward excellence. This is similar to how human life includes medical principles as guidelines to good health. So understood, generosity would be that chosen trait or inclination toward action that steers one to benefit other persons, or indeed anything that is capable of being benefited. (One could be generous toward animals.)

But why would being inclined to benefit *others* amount to a moral virtue, that is, a trait that steers one toward one's own excellence? Is there not a paradox in this? To enhance one's own excellence, one might want to be prudent, even self-interested, but why generous? Would that not be precisely a trait that steers one away from one's own and toward someone else's enhancement of life?[8]

To be able to appreciate that generosity is at once a trait guiding one toward benefiting others and a mode of self-enhancement, or striving for one's own excellence, it is necessary to speak a bit about human nature. But as do so many philosophical topics, the topic of human nature gives rise to numerous questions. And without dealing with those, it will be difficult to avoid seeming arbitrary when discussing human nature.

First, there is the general question of whether one can make clear sense of any reference to the nature of something. That is quite controversial. Many think that the expression "the nature of X" really has no clear referent.

Problems with Defining Human Nature

The nature of government, cancer, or whatever is what *must* be the case for a thing to be what it is. It is the set of attributes that is indispensable for the thing to be what it is. When we ask about what human beings are, we are seeking to know about human nature. And our knowledge of human nature enables us to tell what is part of all human life, not just this or that particular individual's life.

If human nature, for example, is such that it implies generosity as a basic value to human life, that would make a difference to how generosity is understood. Is it merely something some people might embrace while others can just as easily forgo? Or is a human life that lacks the morally generous impulse somehow impoverished, lacking in something essential?

Definitions are attempts to state the attributes of things that are indispensable to their being what they are and that distinguish one thing from other things. But a perplexity arises from the fact that our definitions often change. So, may at one point generosity be part of human life but then stop being necessary to it? And if that is so, what point is there in knowing what makes the thing what it is? After all, what makes it what it is today might change tomorrow. So why should we care about the nature of something if it doesn't give us some measure of stability in our knowledge?

Although in some cases the nature of something does change, if only gradually, it is rarely the case that the nature of something is either fixed forever or fluctuates constantly. So if it turns out that human nature does have an intimate connection with generosity, it isn't likely that this will change any time soon. Our lives would then be lacking something important without generosity.

Generosity and Human Nature

So what is it that's indispensable to being human? The answer will give us some clue as to why generosity, even though a trait inclining us to benefit others, is nevertheless a trait that also enhances our own excellence, that is, makes us better human beings. It is of moral benefit to us, meaning that we are better human beings for having it as a virtue—a result that is of supreme significance for each human being.

Human beings are thinking animals; they have a kind of consciousness or awareness of the world that involves ideas, concepts, theories, explanations, descriptions. And their thinking ability immediately suggests that they can greatly enhance their lives through communication (interaction with others). Just one example should illustrate the point.

Learning from and teaching other persons are made possible by our rational capacity. We can do so much that other animals cannot, because we do not rely only on inborn information (instincts) and experience; we also talk to each other and tell what we know so others can learn it. Education would be impossible without thinking. All that we know would have to be learned from personal experience or inherited genetically.

As we can clearly see, those beings that rely on such restricted learning stay stagnant or petrified throughout their history, from when they emerge in nature to when they become extinct.[9] A cockroach or bee may be a wonder of nature, but from one generation to the next, and on and on, the members of such species do nothing novel. There is no generation gap, with the latest generation inventing all sorts of new practices, institutions, and styles.

But human beings are capable of drawing on the experiences of their elders and building on them without having to spend time repeating them all. That is part of what they can do, their potential. When human beings enter the world, they are nearly wholly ignorant—probably more so than any other animal. But once they open their minds to learning from others, not only the past but also the potential for a new and unheard of future open up for them.

Adam Ferguson made a somewhat similar point when he noted,

> Natural productions are generally formed by degrees. Vegetables grow from a tender shoot, and animals from an infant state. The latter being destined to act, extend their operations as their powers increase: they exhibit a progress in what they perform, as well as in the faculties they acquire. This progress

in the case of man is continued to a greater extent than in that of any other animal. Not only the individual advances from infancy to manhood, but the species itself from rudeness to civilization. . . .

We speak of art as distinguished from nature; but art itself is natural to man. He is in some measure the artificer of his own frame, as well as his fortune, and is destined, from the first age of his being, to invent and contrive . . . whether his motions be rapid or slow, the scenes of human affairs perpetually change in his management: his emblem is a passing stream, not a stagnating pool. We may desire to direct his love of improvement to its proper object, we may wish for stability of conduct; but we mistake human nature, if we wish for a termination of labour, or a scene of repose.[10]

There is a lot more, of course. Aside from educational communication and communion, there are romantic, scientific, entrepreneurial, athletic, and a host of other, more specialized ways that human beings can fulfill their potential through interaction with others.

The idea that a human being is by nature a social animal makes the point clearly enough, given that each human being is a rational animal. The fact of our rational potential opens up many horizons for us. But whether those horizons are going to be explored or neglected depends on what we choose to do. And here is where generosity can be shown to be a virtue. If we are good to others, at least those who deserve it, then that will facilitate our living the kind of life that we are fit—or suited by our nature—to live, which is in large part, of course, a successful social life. The matter is conditional upon our choice of actions, because we are moral agents who need to develop our natural potential in large measure *as a matter of choice*. That is similar to the way one is related to one's talents—one needs to develop them. That's what earns one proper accolades.

If we choose or have cultivated the inclination to act benevolently toward others, who are themselves sociable, then our potential for fulfilling our social capacities will be realized. If we do not, we will remain arrested, truncated, limited in how far we can go in developing ourselves. Generosity is doing what is helpful to other persons, mostly in those circles in which others are reasonably well-known to the generous person. The beneficiary of generous conduct is not, as noted before, benefiting from some duty or obligation—for example, the

10

respect of his rights as a child or a citizen or a party to a contract. Rather, the beneficiary is benefiting from a respect bearing on his individual circumstances—what he might enjoy, need, or want. To know that other people enjoy, need, or want certain things, one must know them reasonably well. (The more institutional forms of generosity have acquired the distinct though somewhat loose designation of charity, philanthropy, or humanitarianism.)

Generosity, then, is a good trait because practicing it makes us more at home with the world. By bestowing upon some others various goods, such as time we have to spare, skills they could use, some article of value, or money, we contribute to the positive upkeep and improvement of the community that can make a more hospitable setting for our life. We may not be making extreme sacrifices by being generous, but we are going beyond the call of duty or obligation. We thus contribute to an atmosphere of congeniality, a fulfilled human life.

Some claim that generosity can be broken into various types, notably economic generosity and generous-mindedness. According to this division, economic generosity would be "giving things whose value is measured in money," while generous-mindedness would involve judging people in ways that treat them kindly, not harshly— as when we do not invoke the highest standards when evaluating the achievements of some friend.[11] Such divisions may have their merit, but they assume a ready differentiation between economic and other values.

There are occasions for such a differentiation—some purpose might be served by it sometimes. But in a general account of generosity, the differentiation seems forced. It seems, indeed, to presuppose a kind of ontological dualism, at least about persons—that they are basically divided in their nature. This dualism would involve assigning to people certain material values with which they may choose to part and various traits, talents, or other attributes that are not material. However, a person may be generous by contributing time, energy, and materials for the well-being of someone else. If someone gives another a favorite lamp, knowing that he would welcome and benefit from it, is that economic generosity alone? Surely the generous individual may have spent time and energy, even talent, obtaining the lamp, and all those are part of what is being contributed.

11

Instead of a division based on an unwarranted dualism, I wish to suggest that there is a continuum stretching between one's belongings and one's time, skills, and so forth, so we have no simple division into material (or economic) and nonmaterial (or noneconomic) values or possessions. Although the framework that encourages that division may be quite popular—paralleling, perhaps, the mind-body, spirit-matter dualism—dividing one's sphere of authority-sovereignty-responsibility along those lines seems unwarranted. That is becoming more and more evident as activities such as organ transplanting, blood giving or selling, and surrogate parenting are becoming more common; "properties" previously thought to be unalienable are being shared with, sold to, or given to other people.

I wish to suggest a different ontological division, one along the lines of permanent and temporary values. People *can* give each other their loyalty and friendship, as well as their cars, stereos, and books. All of those *can* be priced. There might, in short, be a market for them, even if in all decency there ought not to be. As it is sometimes put, there is a price for everything—provided it is for sale. My friendship for another—if it deserves that designation in the first place—may be something I could betray for certain benefits, such as a better position in the company hierarchy. But there is also the fact that I should not do that.

So, trying to sell or trade friendship will involve a serious misunderstanding of the role it plays in human life. It is not, as some economists argue, that friendship and love are just high-priced relationships. (That is what is expressed by the crass notion that "everything has its price.") Clearly, there is a difference between selling out one's friend and trading in one's car. Equating those actions is forced and depends on examples of people with questionable moral character.[12]

Generosity, in my proposed understanding of the concept, involves giving those things that are morally permissible to give, whatever can be provided to others that may be of benefit to them. If it is more time than is due, then it is generous. If it is examination of another's situation with more care than fairness requires, that, too, can be generous. And in some cases, placing monetary value on what is given misses the point, since what is given is not always also available for trade.

But some values are not exchangeable—it would not be generous for me to betray a friend for the good of another friend. The intention of doing good would be vitiated by the bad deed it took to carry it out. The same would be true of attempting to be generous with stolen goods.

Accordingly, some things are designated "generous" ironically. If a professor is said to grade generously, that may suggest, not that he is doing good to some students, but that he is failing to keep up his standards, even that he may have some ulterior motive for slacking off. It is the same when someone in the Mafia is said to be "reasonable," or to make an "offer" that one cannot refuse, or when someone calls it "business" when in fact he is engaged in outright embezzlement. The point is simply to alert everyone to the fact that something is amiss. When we hear "Let us be reasonable here," the speaker may well be asking for undue concessions—which, in the last analysis, would be anything but reasonable.

Virtue and Good Actions

Does what has been said thus far imply that generosity is always going to be something worthwhile, something that invariably vindicates or merits its habituation or cultivation? No. Generosity can be extended indiscriminately. People who are generous may be faulted for that—say, they give too much when they cannot afford it—and thus their generosity will not be a moral virtue on those occasions.

Since generosity is a trait or an inclination, there can be unusual circumstances for which we are ill prepared and in which we will act generously when we should act frugally or prudently. In those cases we could be "generous to a fault." If we are indiscriminate, negligent, or reckless in how we extend ourselves toward others— if we keep giving or helping with what harms others or give to or help undeserving people—then our character trait can no longer qualify as a virtue at all. We will be regarded as gullible, foolhardy, or irrational, albeit perhaps generous. That is why generosity is not always a virtue. So even if we are generous and therefore inclined, in most cases, to do good for those to whom doing good is indeed worthwhile, there can be occasions when we could be generous to a fault—when we could behave generously in such a way that our generosity misfired and ceased to be a virtue.

This suggests that, for generosity to be a virtue, it needs to be accompanied by other moral virtues, which will give generosity its needed limits. And it is clear enough, from the moral perspective that concentrates on virtues, that generosity will not by itself ensure a successful, good human life. We all require other moral virtues. Furthermore, quite possibly it is insufficient for a successful, good human life to rely entirely on our virtues, since they are more or less automatic in the way they guide us. Actions flowing from virtuous traits alone might not be able to deal with unheard of, novel, or surprising situations. Those present to us circumstances we are not familiar with, so any cognitive preparation by which our virtuous actions are nearly automatically triggered would be absent. Indeed, the possibility of being generous to a fault can illustrate the point that some of our virtues may have to be supervised by second thoughts. If, however, one is inclined to share one's good fortune with friends and relatives, and if most of those people are, in fact, deserving of benevolence, one would almost automatically extend oneself toward them. Having habituated or cultivated one's generosity means that one is so inclined, that no on-the-spot deliberation is required to undertake the deeds that will be of benefit to those persons.

Consider now the following somewhat complicated case. One may be confronted with an unknown cousin who is an irresponsible individual—say, a racist who actively promotes his racist ideas and indulges in racist conduct. Yet that is not advertised by him, and to all appearances he is a fine fellow, just as his relatives have proven to be. So upon the occasion when one is ready to share some good fortune—to act in a generous fashion—one may be inclined to include this racist as a beneficiary. And that may indeed make it possible for him to promote racism with greater ease and efficiency. Since such situations are clearly possible and can have unacceptable consequences, one needs other traits of moral character—in short, to live right, one requires several virtues acting, as it were, in concert. Thus generosity by itself will not suffice for one to be a morally good person. One needs prudence, wisdom, courage, honesty, justice, and so forth. That is one reason why integrity, which is the virtue or trait of character of balancing all the other virtues in a proper fashion, is taken to be so vital, a kind of meta-virtue.

Generosity as a Pseudovirtue

David Hume argued that the merits of benevolence consist largely of their service to the public—that is, "that morals must always be handled with a view to public interest."[13] He further noted,

> When the natural tendency of his passions leads him to be serviceable and useful within his sphere, we approve of his character, and love his person, by a sympathy with the sentiments of those who have a more particular connection with him. We are quickly obliged to forget our own interest in our judgments of this kind, by reason of the perpetual contradictions we meet with in society and conversation, from persons that are not placed in the same situation, and have not the same interest with ourselves.[14]

Accordingly, Hume asked, "May it not thence be concluded, that the utility, resulting from the social virtues, forms, at least, a part of their merit, and is one source of that approbation and regard so universally paid to them?"[15] Hume held that it is because of our natural sympathy with those who are like us or are in some agreeable fashion connected with us that we are good to others. He did not, however, embrace what he regarded as the simple theory of Hobbes that self-love underlies the benevolent virtues.[16] He claimed that "a generous man cheerfully embraces an opportunity of serving his friend; because he then feels himself under the dominion of the beneficent affections, nor is he concerned whether any other persons in the universe were ever before actuated by such noble motives, or will ever afterwards prove their influence."[17]

Furthermore, Hume held that "our approbation has, in these cases [where we praise benevolence], an origin different from the prospect of utility and advantage, either to ourselves or to others."[18]

This suggests that the motivation underlying the benevolent virtues, including, especially, generosity, is definitely not the calculated goal of attaining some personal advantage. What, then, is it?

Hume insisted that "from the original frame of our temper, we may feel a desire of another's happiness or good, which, by means of that affection, becomes our own good, and is afterwards pursued, from the combined motives of benevolence and self-enjoyments."[19] What this suggests is that instead of being the result of calculation, benevolence has as its source an innate human sentiment or passion that renders acting benevolently enjoyable.

That conception of generosity is challenging. It accords well with a noncognitive view of good and evil, right and wrong, one, that is, according to which claims about what it is right or wrong for one to do are neither true nor false but express feelings, sentiments, attitudes, dispositions, or the like. It is the beginning of the view that morality is really a branch of personal or social psychology.

Hume made it clear that what is right is not so because it accords with reason—that is, because it is deductively demonstrable by our cognitive faculties that we ought to act in a given way. He appears to have taken this to imply that reason cannot affirm moral truths, although this conclusion restricts the scope of reason, quite unreasonably, to deductive inferences. Now, if we also accept the idea, shared by Hume, that genuine freedom of choice—in the sense of persons causing their own behavior, initiating their own actions— is impossible and we are motivated to do what we do by various psychological dispositions (passions), then this (noncognitive) thesis may indeed be the most cogent view of morality one might hope to arrive at.

But what if we accept, as I have assumed here, that what is right is something that can be known (albeit not always by means of deductive reasoning as distinct from conceptual inference and/or induction from experience or history)? If that is true and generosity is morally right, then generous people gain moral credit for this trait only if at some level—though not perhaps a philosophical or similar intellectual level—they choose it because of its goodness. Hume's view would seem to deprive benevolence, and thus generosity, of moral significance—because generosity is a kind of inborn disposition (though not an instinct, Hume was careful to point out). With the sentiment of benevolence properly honed through approbation, acts based on the "virtue" of generosity would be forthcoming.

That seems to foreshadow B. F. Skinner's conception of morality— wherein both freedom and dignity (which is to say, initiation of action and the consequent credit or discredit accruing to the actor) are denied and at best only good or bad behavior is left. For Hume and those who follow him, morality is not a matter of intentional good conduct. The passions, not reason, underlie the actions that are deemed good, and the explanation for their being deemed good is that they are socially agreeable. That sort of generosity, then— even if disinterested because not motivated by self-love—is not a moral character trait but a psychological propensity.

That is not the kind of generosity that is being discussed here. No doubt, it exists—someone can be generous because of an emotional or *accidentally habituated or cultivated* sympathy with others.

This is a familiar motive for action. Often enough the behavior involved is difficult to distinguish from bona fide morally significant generosity. But the motivation of such helpful conduct serves to distinguish it from generosity as understood here—it is done from necessity, not choice.

The question can be raised, of course, whether the kind of generosity we are supposing to be a moral virtue could even exist. If the analysis of morality that Hume and his followers embrace is correct—if in the end we act benevolently as a result of an inborn propensity or sentiment that serves the public interest—then the kind of generosity I have thought is possible between human beings would have to be deemed bogus, impossible. More than that, the moral psychology that serves as the background for the Humean view has some drastic implications.

There is no clear evidence in history that human beings generally exhibit the sentiment of benevolence. Indeed, the evidence is mixed—callousness, meanness, and lack of compassion are as evident as generosity, kindness, and charity toward others. The very idea of living either virtuously or viciously is predicated on the absence of innate prompters for either one. Those are matters of choice. If they are not, then there is really nothing blameworthy about being mean, nasty, hostile, or suspicious, even where no objective reason for those sentiments exists. Blaming racist sentiments would be just as pointless as praising the sentiment of humanity or congeniality.

Furthermore, mere sentiment is never really the issue, is it? What is wanted is well-motivated, well-intended action, something that one would hope turns into a habit. Too often, sound policy is undermined by the emphasis on nice sentiment. The contemporary phrase "tough love" is used to call attention to the idea that attitudes other than gushing sentiment can serve to benefit people who are in need; however, as we shall see, there is good evidence that the current inclination to profess grave concern, compassion, feeling—"I feel your pain"—encourages a kind of mindlessness about what will actually do the most good.[20]

It seems to me, accordingly, that the Humean account of ethics and the subsequent positivist account (i.e., the moral psychological account) falter for a variety of reasons, among them those just mentioned. Most fundamentally, they conflict with the evident fact that human beings make choices before they initiate their most significant actions. If one denies this, too many facts of human life remain unexplained. Clearly, scientific objectivity and independence would have to go, since we would all be merely doing what we have to do, not what we judge is most appropriate, even when it concerns the discovery of truth.

Second, much of the variability of human life—be it superficially identified as simply cultural, ethnic, racial, sexual, or national—would go unexplained. Generation after generation, across the globe, experiences novelty, innovation, invention, and so forth, all of which are manifest in what we now see as the immense variety of cultures, religions, ethnicities. That seems best explained by reference to the capacity of human beings to engage in original thought and action and is to be distinguished from the relative lack of change in the lives of other living species, most of which simply carry on with the activities of previous generations until some environmentally induced or random alteration occurs, usually quite apart from the individual animal's or plant's causal—let alone intentional—influence.

Third, even to recommend determinism seems to deny it, since it implies that one ought to change one's mind on the topic. But "ought" implies "can," and that means that the person considering the determinist's argument is presumed to be free to change his mind. There is also the fact that we are aware of our acts of original choice. We make note of this when we blame ourselves for having missed an opportunity—"Damn it! I didn't think to do that!" Introspective evidence may not be conducive to simple positivism, but in the richer framework of human understanding—as well as in reports to doctors about the conditions of our bodies (as in "Doctor, it hurts here")—there is no way to do without it. Finally, there are now arguments from within psychophysics maintaining that free choice is a distinctive capacity of the human form of consciousness.[21]

With such an array of grounds, as well as the difficulties involved in the epistemological underpinnings of the determinism we find in Hume's and other positivists' view of the matter, it seems that we need not be detained further by trying to rebut the Humean account of morality and, thus, of generosity.

Adam Smith on Generosity and Humanity

Adam Smith, who was close to Hume both personally and philosophically, proposed yet another conception of generosity, one that is a bit closer to the popular understanding of this virtue. He told us, "We never are generous except when in some respect we prefer some other person to ourselves, and sacrifice some great and important interest of our own to an equal interest of a friend or of a superior."[22] So then Smith considered "the man who exposes his life to defend that of his friend which he judges to be of more importance"[23] an especially clear case of a generous individual.

The present understanding of generosity disputes that line of thinking about this moral virtue. Smith seemed to believe that generosity is not a self-enhancing virtue—although by linking it to preferring one's friend to oneself, Smith's analysis did contain a certain measure of self-regard. After all, satisfying one's preference counts as serving one's interest, especially in much economic analysis of human behavior.

If it is recalled, though, that Smith worked with a conception of the human being that is basically distinct from what is assumed here, the difference between the understanding of generosity exhibited by Smith and that of the present work will make sense. To Smith, the passions, or sentiments, are prior to human rationality—reason is, in Hume's terms, "the slave of the passions." So, human beings are not by nature—by what they are as beings in the world—essentially and primarily rational or even social. It is no accident that the neoclassical economic tradition, in which *Homo economicus* figures so prominently, derives much of its understanding of human life from Smith. In that framework, it is a matter of calculation whether one will engage in social relationships—Robinson Crusoe decided to be social when he began to trade with Friday; he could just as easily have decided not to.

Generosity could not, in that framework, arise *naturally* in human beings or be *by nature* a part of their lives—which is to say, be properly suited to how they ought to live. It is not part and parcel of the fully realized human life to exhibit generosity. That kind of thinking is alien to how Smith and his followers think about human life (even if they do employ the terminology, as when Smith speaks of "natural liberty"). The very idea of a "fully realized human being" makes little sense within the general philosophical framework in which Smith worked (wherein talk about "the nature of X" or "the essence of X" is at most a loose figure of speech, without philosophical grounding) since that idea makes sense only within a teleological understanding of life. By "teleological" understanding I mean one that conceives of the ends or goals of life as serving to explain why a being behaves this or that way or possesses this or that faculty or organ.

That may seem just a technical point, but it has serious ramifications. One of the concerns in contemporary Western culture is that a certain kind of individualism makes it impossible to have smoothly functioning communities. This is the gist of the complaint about the "me generation," and even the subsequent alienated "generation X." It is also at the heart of the complaint of many communitarians that liberal individualism is "atomistic." They argue that there cannot be a smooth, sensible, or rational link between the individual and the community within the prevailing, modern conception of human nature. According to that conception, every relationship the individual has is a matter of rational calculation about whether relating to this or that person or community serves his desires, satisfies his preferences.

Some efforts are afoot, of course, to establish the social aspect of human life as having a fairly firm basis in the *Homo economicus* tradition—the talk of "tit for tat," reciprocity, harmony of interests, and so forth is an example.[24] The idea is that, when people interact, their goodwill toward each other is predicated on some rational expectation of reciprocity. Thus, they have a strong incentive to relate to others. The expectation may, incidentally, be generalized, even unselfconscious. Nevertheless, it forms the basis for "goodwill," including generous, kind, benevolent conduct. Yet, when one complains about people of the me generation, one is not lamenting that those people are insufficiently aware of the advantages to them that others can provide—which is what tit for tat stresses. No, the complaint centers on the lack of a basic embrace of others as part of one's life, a realization that one is intimately connected to at least some others whose well-being will be a natural concern.

The understanding of human nature on which I rely makes this possible. Without the recognition that other persons matter to oneself, the capacity of reason cannot be realized in full measure. Thus, generosity within this school is neither a matter of calculated self-interest nor one of altruistic self-sacrifice.

Furthermore, with that understanding of the virtue of generosity, it becomes clear that generosity needs to be voluntary, a matter of one's own realization of one's whole self, that it cannot be achieved by coercion, by one's being regimented to behave well toward others. Even when one is tempted to neglect this virtue, it is still up to oneself to recover from such negligence and to fulfill one's responsibility to be a virtuous person—not, however, merely because it is one's duty, in the sense of a chore one owes others, but because it means living successfully as a good human being. And that, in the best sense of the word, is a selfish task. Any act or public policy that robs one of the chance to fulfill that task is, in the last analysis, demoralizing and cannot help to improve human community.

Some people, of course, dispute this, and we will consider such opposition throughout this work. Let me just point to a recent frontal attack on it by Robert P. George. George notes that "the proponent of any particular putative moral right to do moral wrong will need to adduce some ground for the claim that it is morally impermissible for the law to forbid the immoral act or abolish the immoral institution in question."[25] We may assume that George has in mind such things as failing to be charitable when one should be and running a gambling hall where many gamble who should not do so. George says, correctly, that "it will not do to cite baldly the moral right to perform the act or have the institution as the ground of this moral impermissibility."[26]

The reason for the impermissibility of legislating morality as George proposes is that to intervene in the wrong act or to ban the immoral institution will thwart the moral agency of the choosing and acting person and rob him or her of the opportunity to do the right thing on his or her own initiative. The same is the case with institutions that can be or are morally objectionable. To change them, to reform them, would be a moral achievement, which is something that would be impossible on the part of those responsible for their existence, if they were banned by law.[27]

In a recent essay Douglas Rasmussen makes the point as follows: "To say that X-ing is morally right or good and ought to be done does not, in and of itself, imply that X-ing ought to be legally (coercively) required. Nor does saying that X-ing is morally wrong or bad and ought not to be done, in and of itself, imply that X-ing ought to be legally (coercively) prohibited. Something being right or wrong does not, by itself, carry any implications about what should be a concern of the political/legal order."[28]

George, however, argues that the moral wrongness of conduct may provide a reason (i.e., a possible rational motive) for interfering in someone's performance of that conduct, but there may be competing reasons not to interfere. George then considers what those reasons might be, and it is in those competing reasons that he considers the debate between the liberal and the conservative (communitarian) to lie.

But George's description of the situation begs all the important questions from a liberal point of view. First, to say that something may be a possible rational motive for conduct is to say that it may be a means of action toward some end, and "rational motive" is explained by reference to the end. Yet this is the very issue that is being debated between George and the liberals: what should the end of state, political, legal action be? It is possible that the end of state, political, legal action is not human flourishing or "the moral" but something else; and, if so, the moral wrongness of an action would not be a possible rational motive for interference.

George also ignores the possibility that the relation of the moral to the political might not be direct or isomorphic and thus not all moral concerns would necessitate political concern.

Second, abstractly considered, the moral wrongness of an action may be a basis for state, political, legal action, and it may also *not* be a basis for such action. To decide which, one needs to know what allows one to move from the moral to the state, political, legal.

Third, it now appears that the point about a failure of the moral, in and of itself, to imply the state, political, legal stands unrefuted. In short, simply because something is morally wrong, it does not follow that it should be legally banned—for example, yellow journalism may be morally objectionable, yet it ought to be given protection (by, say, the First Amendment of the U.S. Constitution).

Fourth, we see here why the anarchist challenge to the legitimacy of the state is an important one: it reminds us not to assume that the moral is all there is to the political.[29] What is probably much more sensible is that the scope of the moral is far greater than that of the political, precisely because, if politics were to exhaust the moral domain, that would eliminate the possibility of bona fide personal responsibility, the chance of human beings to do right and wrong, to become good or bad, on their own.

But we will return later to the broader sociopolitical implications of the nature of human generosity.

22

Generosity vis-à-vis Other Virtues

A precondition of the possibility of generosity as a virtue is the existence of moral priorities. Generous is what one ought to be after being just. Virtues form a hierarchy. For example, fulfilling one's moral responsibilities to one's family takes priority over being generous to a neighbor. Put differently, parental duty, fraternity, and more generally, integrity, for example, come before generosity. Kindness and compassion would come after generosity. A needy stranger, for example, should be thought of in emergencies, while the hardship of a friend should quickly elicit generosity. Without, for example, the wisdom to be cautious about how one regards strangers and the prudence to forbear jumping to prejudicial and thus very likely faulty conclusions about others, one's other virtues will have been, as it were, misspent.

If one did not first attend to one's primary moral responsibilities, such as taking proper care of one's children and attending fully to one's professional duties, being prudent or generous or courageous could amount to a kind of careless indulgence. Since the virtues of a person are second nature, they cannot be counted on to take care of all of one's moral tasks. So there is a limit to how far one may rely on just one virtuous trait; for example, as noted above, one would have to be characterized as generous to a fault if one benefited someone who was evidently "evil" or made contributions to causes one simply could not afford because one's own children or other responsibilities would be neglected. Such generosity would trail off into recklessness, even indiscretion. (Discretion is a species of wisdom.) A foolhardy generosity would seem to be possible, one that is misguided and thus produces not benefit but harm and guides one into an inappropriate, unsuitable kind of life.

There are several ways in which one's generosity might misfire. One could be wrong-headedly generous even to those who apparently are the intended beneficiaries. If, acting on my inclination to extend myself and what is mine toward others, I generously give some cigarettes to a teenager, that may hurt the young person and fail to be genuinely benevolent. Yet the trait that inclines me to such conduct may still be regarded as generosity. What I lack, again, is some other virtue or moral discipline, such as forethought or vigilance. The lack of one kind of moral attribute may have a deleterious effect upon my ability to properly exercise some other trait that would ordinarily be a virtue.

Clearly, at least morally worthwhile generosity is a good thing because of our social nature. That is why we specify "generous to a fault," since ordinarily no such results of generosity would be expected. Generosity as a general trait could be relied upon to incline one toward benevolent behavior and even guarantee such behavior under familiar circumstances. Yet there are exceptions to general principles of conduct, including moral dilemmas, where such a trait is not fully reliable as a guide to moral behavior. Accordingly, while generosity is on the whole a virtue, it needs to coexist with other virtues to lead one to act ethically, that is, to be good on the whole. All this is said in the context of an understanding that virtues are traits that guide one toward such conduct as will produce success in human life, that is, to a life that can be judged a good one. And since single virtues never ensure that result, it is not surprising that single virtues, without the coexistence of others, may even incline one toward occasional actions that are morally improper or wrong.

Perhaps an analogy would be useful here to further clarify the issues involved. There are general rules of good driving taught by most driving schools and driving instructors. Those rules are generally appropriate to the kind of driving conditions that face one in one's vicinity, where one is presumed to be doing one's driving. And we expect that a good driver will acquire or cultivate driving habits or traits that are suitable to success in this area of his life. They will enable the person to reach his destination safely, directly, and punctually. But driving about even in the most familiar vicinity will at times present one with unforeseen circumstances, and those may require modification of the general principles of competent driving. A good driver will be alert for such circumstances. Such a driver will not depend entirely on habituated or cultivated traits but will employ a measure of discipline to look out for the possibility of having to adapt quickly to new problems.

In a similar vein, general moral virtues are not by themselves sufficient to guide one to the best kind of living, inasmuch as living involves many unforeseen circumstances for which general traits cannot be cultivated. Here there is perhaps no general trait at all that can be called upon. One may simply have to keep things in focus and see what is called for. Keeping in focus may itself be a kind of trait that some persons can cultivate for themselves. But since it involves energetic attention, which needs to be chosen, it may be distinct from generosity and other virtues that incline one toward specific kinds of behavior.

We could spend considerable time exploring just what other forms of good conduct are needed for generosity to function consistently as a virtue. But rather than set out all of the possible combinations of virtues and circumstances, it is likely to be more fruitful to ask whether there may indeed be one overriding general form of conduct, as hinted at above, that needs to be carried out all the time so that a person can be prepared to cope with unfamiliar problems.

Is There a Cardinal Virtue?

We have already seen that prudence is a candidate for another virtue a human being ordinarily requires. The best candidate for some general, overriding virtue is what has been called right reason, rationality, or, perhaps, wisdom.

In traditional Christian moral philosophy, the four cardinal virtues are prudence, justice, temperance, and fortitude. In some ways this seems quite right—first one needs to take care of one's life in general, then one needs to be respectful of others' dignity, then one must live in measured ways, and finally one must have the backbone to stick by all these virtues. "Right reason," or "rationality" or "good sense"—prudence in the sense of practical rationality, thinking things through before one acts, whether a long or short time before one takes the action in question—appears to be the most vital of the virtues, since it is the first thing one must have to guide oneself through life with reasonable chances for success as far as one's overall conduct is concerned. Right reason is nothing less than the act of keeping in conceptual mental focus—or, to put it less imposingly, having an alert mind. Since this is the locus of human freedom of choice—everyone not crucially incapacitated can choose to be alert or not to be alert—that indeed is the central moral act.

We are not embarking here on a full discussion of the virtues or morality, or on a catalog of all the virtues. I mention the issue of what is morally most important in life only because it is necessary for us to observe that the various specific virtues may not be adequate for guiding us toward a successful or good human life. Something else, some supervisory, guiding virtue, would now and then have to stand ready to help out when the others were not adequate. And when one considers this from the viewpoint of common sense, it sounds right, does it not? We must rely on good habits and practices to get us through our days with reasonable success, but we must also be alert enough always to meet possible emergencies. (The driving analogy can again serve to make this evident.)

Generosity at a Glance

What can we say now about generosity? It is a trait that can be cultivated, and it inclines one toward benevolence toward others— doing what is good for them as a matter of second nature. It depends on familiarity with the beneficiaries of generous conduct if it is a habitual guide in one's life. It can go astray, now and then, when the evidence that would usually bring it to the fore—that is, when one is in the position to share good fortune or reward hard work— misguides one to benefit someone who is undeserving, to extend to someone what in fact is harmful, or to neglect or sacrifice other things that one should value more highly. Generosity, like other virtues, is not by itself reliable as a guide to action. It requires other virtues, as well as a kind of moral monitoring or supervision by the person coping with unfamiliar tasks.

2. Dimensions of Generosity: Private, Social, and Political

Contexts of Generosity

Probably almost everyone is generous some of the time—the pedestrian who stops to give directions to a stranger, the merchant who discusses with a customer where a rare item might be located, the doctor who gives advice at a cocktail party, and so forth. We have encountered the generous lawyer, educator, tailor, and psychoanalyst—folks who lend a hand quite naturally, unselfconsciously. People take time they could perhaps use for something they prefer, because they find that others would benefit from something they can do for them.

If it is just a bit of help that is needed, we are often quite indiscriminate as to who shall receive it, barring, of course, knowingly giving it to undeserving persons. Thus, the merchant will not advise the hold-up man about where his next target might be found, nor do we offer help to purse snatchers as they run from the constable. Rather, we help the authorities, assuming, as it is mostly reasonable to do, that their objective is a worthy one. (An exception is when we hide our Jewish neighbor from the *Schutzstaffel* in Hitler's Germany, at some considerable risk to ourselves, knowing well enough whose side we should be on. Those who help the authorities in such communities are properly seen as vicious, complicit in the perpetration of a gross injustice. Those who fail to provide aid are contributing to injustice and bear some guilt for viciousness— neglecting, as they do, the support of justice.)

In this chapter, we will look at the various contexts of generosity that are open to most people and examine just how that virtue manifests itself in those contexts. While there are many special contexts we could focus on—for example, relations among colleagues in a given profession or at a given institution (firm, university, division, department, team)—I plan to concentrate on three broad areas: the private, the social, and the political. By private I mean the sphere that touches on one's personal, romantic, family, and fraternal concerns—the intimate dimension of one's life. Of course, those are already encumbered by social elements. Yet what distinguishes them as private is that the people one relates to in those contexts are concerned with one's personal life, with oneself as an individual—not as doctor, teacher, taxicab driver, athlete, artist, or trading partner—and one's own concern with those persons is not confined to the "utilitarian" dimensions of life.

By social I mean the vast sphere of relationships one can have with others in one or another of the vast manifestations of humanity—persons in their roles as teachers, coaches, airline attendants, butchers, priests, postal service employees, dental hygienists, service station attendants, psychiatrists, trumpet players, veterinarians, publishers, philosophers, biologists, economists, news reporters, and so forth. Those are all individuals we might relate to and with whom situations might arise in which generosity could play a role. It is instructive to inquire just how the generosity of a person would manifest itself in that broader social context.

There is also the political dimension of our lives, one that pertains to the upholding of the principles of our legal community. Here we are concerned mainly with whether the basic framework of our society is adequately taken care of, administered, and maintained. What, if any, bearing does generosity have on this dimension of our lives? And how does politics bear on the prospect of generosity within a human community?

I will take a close look at each of these areas with an eye to seeing how generosity is affected by or related to it.

Generosity in Private

It is possible for one to be generous in a variety of types of circumstances. Although public discussions tend to center on generosity that reaches beyond the borders of one's private life—that is, organized "charity" and philanthropy—that does not make generosity in the private context morally irrelevant.[1] No pundits sing praises of the generosity of one's aunt or sister; yet in the actual lives of people, that is just the sort of manifestation of generosity that is of vital importance. And while not everyone gains a public reputation for his moral character, including his generosity, the actual moral quality of the lives of those who engage in private generosity could be every bit as noble as that of the lives of some prominently praised public figure.

Furthermore, it is also in private that generosity can often misfire. While from the viewpoint of other people one's generosity to a fault might not be a severe failure, as far as one's personal responsibilities are concerned, it clearly can be. If a husband becomes too enamored of stray dogs and neglects his wife, or a father extends himself too far to reach out toward a special cause such as wildlife preservation and thus neglects his duties to his children, that could be generosity gone astray. To adequately appreciate the nature of generosity, then, it would help to examine how it manifests itself in private lives.

Generosity and the Family

For most of us, it is members of our family who first make generosity possible. A brother may take extra time to play with his sister, not looking for thanks but simply knowing of her desire for a playmate. He goes out of his way, not because his parents taught him that this is how good brothers behave, but because he has chosen to be alert to the circumstances in which he can be supportive. Later in life, the same brother may find his sister in need of help with the children so she can spend some private hours with her husband— they have so little opportunity for that kind of thing these days, what with both of them working at new jobs. The brother can tell how precious those private hours would be, so he spontaneously volunteers to stay with the kids for an entire Saturday afternoon and evening, forgoing the chance to play his regular 18 holes of golf that day.

Again, the brother does not do that because of some injunction or rule that he recalls and in terms of which he disciplines himself to be unquestioningly giving or charitable. Rather, he understands his sister's need and has a genuine feeling for her and wants, as a matter of his personal desire and inclination, to help her out. Those are cases of generosity within the family. They could be much more serious in substance—loaning money for a down payment on a home, letting some family member make use of the summer home for a badly needed vacation, not insisting on immediate repayment of a debt, or footing the bill for a major operation. As long as helpful deeds are spontaneous, natural, not the result of a battle of conscience—"What is my duty here? What must I do to meet my obligations as a member of the family?"—they are acts of generosity. They testify to the person's having the kind of character that is at home with his community, with the presence of intimate others in his life who have needs and wants he can often satisfy and will take joy in satisfying.

There is little self-sacrifice or net loss in such generosity—the generous person in question would not hear of being described as someone who made a sacrifice, who gave up something of great value to him to do something of value only to the beneficiary. Rather, the generous person would regard that as something he wanted to do, found worth doing, indeed did not even give much thought to but went ahead and did as a matter of course. Yet the result benefited another person, one who means a lot to the agent of the generous act. The generous act was not done to win favors or to express some admiration or adoration, as it would be in romantic love. No, the generous act is a matter of giving without vested interest as a motive, not even the most legitimate vested interest, namely, to express one's deepest love.

A generous brother or sister or aunt has a trait of character that manifests itself in devotion to the welfare of the other, an interest that almost breaks down the distinction between oneself and the other, that defies any suggestion of possible conflict of interest. The mind of a generous person is attuned to the signals that communicate the needs and wants of those intimate others who may be the beneficiaries of his generosity. But how would a generous person be able to act in a way that distinguishes between those who should be helped and those who would abuse help? Is the generous person a highly vulnerable, gullible individual who can be exploited endlessly? There is, as we have already noted, the possibility of being generous to a fault. Generous people will not be wisely generous unless they possess other virtues in addition to generosity.

Generosity and Friends

Can one be generous to friends? Friendship may indeed be characterized in part in terms of friends' generosity toward each other. While much more is required in friendship, those who do not act generously toward each other could be friends only if their circumstances made generosity toward anyone impossible. Thus, if friends found themselves in situations that demanded relentless professionalism—say, while they were performing brain surgery or fighting fires—no room for generosity would exist for them. And if friends became so destitute that all their time and energy were taken up by mere survival efforts, again, generosity would play no or at most a minuscule role in their relationship.[2] But it is questionable whether ordinary friendships could even be sustained in such settings—only the deepest kind would survive in such circumstances.

Generally, moral virtues have limits. In a state of siege, one cannot reasonably expect that persons will observe certain moral principles, ones that are not primary. It may be expected that prime moral principles ought never to be violated or forgotten, but that is not possible with subsidiary, second- or third-order, virtues. That is clear when we come to such valued traits as courtesy or politeness. Of course, those border on being mere manners, not morals at all, although if one is discourteous or impolite toward certain people, that can be a moral fault. Generosity may itself not be a prime virtue—certainly within certain ethical systems it is not. Adam Smith made the point well when he noted, "Beneficence, therefore, is less essential to the existence of society than justice. Society may subsist, though not in the most comfortable state, without beneficence; but the prevalence of injustice must utterly destroy it."[3] It is very likely that this is also true in relation to private or interpersonal conduct: it is more important to show due respect for others' basic rights than to extend to them a helping hand.

In this monograph I am not going to defend fully any particular moral theory, so we will not have a conclusive discussion of how imperative it is to be generous or how high a moral virtue generosity is. Nonetheless, it is plain enough that ethical principles are not all on the same footing—some are more important than others, say, honesty versus punctuality, to use an easy example.

Nevertheless, it is evident enough that the virtue of generosity is not the ultimate or first virtue of human life.[4] So what we are considering is whether and how friendship involves generosity where generosity is possible. Actually, generosity between friends is perhaps the most simple to understand. Friends are chosen relations; in fact, friendship is probably the most deliberate of the human relationships one is likely to have in one's life. Romantic relationships, in contrast, may often eventuate as the consequence of feelings one is able to resist acting on only with some difficulty—hence the expression "falling in love." The falling alludes to an appreciable element of involuntariness in the formation of such a relationship. In contrast, friends are made. The allusion here is to a deliberate or at least intentional process. One makes a friend or forms a friendship. And that can make clear from the outset that there will be strong benevolent feelings involved, generating firm benevolent actions.

Yet at the same time, friendship is also a suspect sphere for generosity. There is the high probability in each case that one extends oneself *solely* because of one's own good feeling or satisfaction about having and keeping a friend, only, in short, to please oneself, not primarily because one is thinking of the well-being of the other person. But that is only an apparent obstacle to regarding friendship as a sound and valid basis for generosity. If generosity is a type of spontaneous benevolence toward another, and if such spontaneous benevolence has its ultimate moral grounding in one's nature as a social being, then within friendship, generosity would seem to be very much on home ground.[5] The affinity one has with a friend is very close and natural in that a person sees a friend, as Aristotle put it, as "another self." And there is nothing deliberately calculating about the regard one has for such another self; an act or an attitude may be rational without being deliberate or calculated. The resulting generosity is then a trait of character, not the suspicious gift giving of commercial or political association where the objective is some specific gain one expects to receive in return. (If one sets out to give simply so as to feel good about oneself, such giving is, in principle, no different from giving in order to obtain some benefit in return.)

Does this contradict the earlier idea that friends are made? Does one, after all, fall into friendship, as it were, inadvertently? That is worth some scrutiny because if we understand how the process might be both natural and intentional, a crucial aspect of not just friendship but also generosity as a virtue may unfold for us. Addressing that question requires some investigation of how character traits become a part of oneself—whether they are accidental, imposed from outside, or amount to a type of achievement for which credit or praise may well be due to a person.

The character one has come to possess, contrary to what is somewhat ambiguously suggested by John Rawls, does not depend "in large part upon fortunate family and social circumstances for which he can claim no credit."[6] It is to a considerable degree self-made, self-cultivated, self-initiated, self-honed, and often self-destroyed or self-undermined, even if the process is not always self-monitored or reflected upon. Of course, in childhood the example and instruction of others will make a big difference, yet not without the gradually increasing cooperation of the child.

This much follows from our earlier observation that human beings can make basic significant choices about their lives and that morality can be concerned only with aspects of their behavior that involve choice.

Clearly, the intelligibility of moral discourse presupposes that human beings, or moral agents in general, have the capacity for making basic choices, are free to initiate some of their conduct. Even to urge us—as does John Rawls—to be fair and not allow any unequal holdings to accrue to those with advantages that others do not possess (unless that improves the condition of the worst off in society) is to implicitly acknowledge that we do make choices. How else could we conceive of changing our minds and directing our behavior toward what Rawls considers fairness? How else could we conceive of at least snubbing (or even punishing) those who would refuse the invitation—or moral imperative, if it is that—to fairness? Why, in short, do we find it morally wrong for people, indeed blameworthy of them, to be unfair or to support unfair institutions? If they cannot help what they are doing, if they are fashioned to be as they are solely by their social circumstances or family backgrounds, there is nothing for which to blame them and all is as it has to be, with no culprit or victim and no injustice anywhere. Rawlsian ideas about moral character undermine the moral force of Rawls's own position.

The capacity for free choice is all that is assumed in the view that character is self-made, not produced by forces over which a person has no control. And that is what makes sense of the idea that while one is (largely) responsible for one's character, one also lays the foundation for friendship with certain others properly situated (e.g., accessible). Once it is understood that one is responsible for one's character—never mind that this is not true of much else about one (e.g., temperament, age, color, and ethnic origins)—it should be evident enough why the bond of friendship may be either directly or indirectly created.

A friendship is the consequence of being who one is and the friend's being who he or she is. And from that it makes sense to conclude that the attitude of generosity that flows from friendship, though personal, is also very clearly and naturally other-oriented. The other person is simply a natural beneficiary of one's life and actions, because of both who one is and who the other is. Generosity flowing from friendship, then, is a case of bona fide benevolence toward the friend, even though it is intimately tied to oneself, one's personal character.

Individuality and Virtues

To conduct oneself morally, to follow the dictates of the virtues and other ethical principles, is to choose to live well. That choice may be influenced by other people—parents, neighbors, heroes, leaders, ministers, friends, and so forth. But in the last analysis, *it is morally significant only if it is the choice of the agent who is engaging in the moral conduct at issue.*

While in most spheres of action men and women live by other than total self-reliance, in their moral lives—or, as it is put at times, in their soul of souls—they must rely on themselves. Here is where they come off as better or worse people. Within some domain or sphere of action, virtually everyone enjoys some measure of personal sovereignty, even in the limit case of a totalitarian system. People still own some valued items and govern some of their important actions, if only unofficially, without legal protection. It is when they make decisions about what is theirs, decisions that they do not have imposed upon them by others or by circumstances, that they place themselves in the position of moral agent.

For moral agency to be widely possible, there must be a certain demarcation of different spheres of authority between individuals who live in society, at least once they have reached adulthood. For individuals to exercise and develop moral agency, there must be individual sovereignty, and that sovereignty requires some measure of constancy—usually secured through the instrument of law.

Moral agency and its corresponding social prerequisite of individual sovereignty do not require actual isolation, as some might imagine, but only an awareness of where one's sphere of moral jurisdiction lies. Within that sphere, one is responsible for one's choices. And if that sphere is invaded, moral responsibility becomes obscured—a type of tragedy of the commons is generated, just as when people don't know where the physical limits of their jurisdictions lie and start getting in each other's way without actually choosing to do so. Cooperation, friendship, neighborliness, and so forth all gain their human quality from being in part a product of ever so subtle yet individual choice, of ever so tacit and personal decision. Basic individual human rights spell out the conditions for cooperation (and needed mutual compliance) among strangers, or nonintimate adults. They are principles that spell out the basic, most fundamental moral requirements of human community life. (They are derived from more basic moral principles that spell out how human beings ought to live as individuals in or out of society.)

Generosity in the Social Fabric

People take part in numerous projects that may not seem to be of direct personal significance to them. They champion the arts, sciences, wildlife, historical preservation, antique cars, old movies, intramural sports, the moral education of the young, promulgation of religious beliefs, and so forth. Although when looked at from the perspective of a life span, the success of those causes may be to their benefit, contributing to their advancement will not usually provide an immediate payoff. Rather, one is disposed, as a matter of one's character, to see to it that certain causes are furthered and those who make their success likely are given support.

Here is where generosity as a distinctive part of one's social life manifests itself. When one provides support, help, or assistance so as to promote the sort of causes in the above list, neither with the expectation of some direct benefit or self-satisfaction ("I did it so as to feel good about myself") nor to fulfill an obligation or duty ("It is required of me to support the environmental movement"), one manifests generosity on the social front.

It is, moreover, a moral failure, not a legal or political one, to stand apart from all such social involvements, unless one is facing dire straits.

Speaking generally, it is a mistake of our time to ignore the social dimension of human life or, more accurately, to conflate it with the political or legal. Thus, those who speak of the social responsibility of, say, corporations often mean not what corporations ought to do about their social surroundings but what the law should make them do or what public policy should be enacted to get them to do. The same holds for lamentations about people's lack of generosity, charity, kindness, or compassion—many such lamentations immediately entail calling upon the government to get us all to be more generous, charitable, and the like. Unlike moral responsibilities vis-à-vis various aspects of our society—religion, science, athletics, education, and the like—legal obligations involve imperatives that can be enforced coercively. And those are necessarily limited in a society of free and responsible persons. Moral virtues such as generosity, courage, and prudence must be practiced voluntarily—one is not *obligated to others* to act on them. They are binding on one as a matter of one's own choice to live a full human life, not because failing to act on them would invade another's moral space or sphere of jurisdiction.[7]

We have moral responsibilities to others, not because those who might benefit are entitled, but because of our choice to live human lives within the company of others. And if we fulfill those responsibilities simply out of fear of coercion, we do not deserve any moral credit. In the terms made famous by Immanuel Kant, we cease to be "ends in ourselves," to be autonomous, sovereign persons, if moral virtues are dictated to us.

Generosity, as are other moral virtues, is due from us because we have a commitment to ourselves to live fully human lives. But it is not due from us because others have a right to it. Those who insist that this is the justification of moral generosity unjustifiably politicize all of human life. They propose to make all of human life a matter of regimentation from above, with little room left for life's greatest task, the achievement of the moral life of a responsible human being through our own free choice.

Politics and Generosity

Rights as Social Guidelines

Individuals have rights to life, liberty, and property—which is to say that in society no one may murder, kidnap, assault, steal from, or extort from another person.[8] Those are negative rights—they impose on others the enforceable obligation *not to act* in certain ways, not to invade other people's private domains. (The operative term here is "private," meaning that some way of distinguishing "mine" from "thine" needs to be at work here, and the theory of natural private-property rights serves this purpose.) Positive rights, in turn, are supposed to spell out duties to provide some service to the rightsholder. But positive rights are not basic rights. They arise from the explicit or implicit consent of individuals—for example, from contracts or from reproduction. To appreciate the difference, one might consider that it is no virtue not to kill, assault, rape, or extort from others—it goes without saying that we need to abstain from such actions—whereas providing help to one in need would normally qualify as a morally virtuous act. The reason is that prohibitions of such conduct are a social prerequisite for people to act morally, to achieve a morally good life. If we could be subjected with impunity to murder, assault, kidnapping, robbery, and their various nuanced implications, we would in effect have no life of our own to live. We would be at the mercy of others' decisions; we would need permission to act (just as we do once something is treated as a public matter).

So, positive rights transform what are cases of moral virtue into cases of coerced obligation for which no moral credit is to be earned. They are also impossible to secure equally for all, without the protection of the rights of some people trampling the rights of others. Unfairness, then, is built into the very idea of positive basic rights.

It is not in order here to defend the claim that basic human individual rights are negative. I have argued that elsewhere.[9] But a few points need to be offered to explain the position, since there is in our time considerable sympathy for the view that basic rights ought really to include some positive rights, for example, rights to health care, social security, housing, nutrition, and education.

Even if those benefits might warrant public provision, they are not basic rights. They cannot be basic because they beg the question of what kind of impositions, if any, may be placed upon others in one's interaction with them. If we may force others to educate our children, to feed us, to provide us with health care, why not with their one eye when we are blind, their one kidney when both ours are damaged, their entire life if we need it badly enough? And if we are entitled to their support, when are they entitled to ours, and who has priority in all this?

Such positive rights constrain, arbitrarily, the jurisdiction of individuals in the sphere of choosing or neglecting to choose to do what is right, and they introduce a state of perpetual war within societies that aim to provide them protection.[10] Negative basic rights—which is to say the rights not to be killed, assaulted, and so forth—amount to placing borders around individuals as human beings, within which they are the sovereign judges in charge of what is to be done. Forbidding others to violate such rights does not amount to dictating to them how to live and treats them as the kind of beings they are, human. It is for this reason they were dubbed "natural" rights in the first place, because they pertain to the conditions required in society for living a properly human life.

The reason basic rights are negative is that their function is to provide adult persons with a sphere of moral jurisdiction and to alert others who want to benefit from social life to the scope of that sphere: if you live among people and want, as you properly should, to reap the benefits of such a life, certain basic principles need to be heeded. Basic negative rights, prohibitions of certain acts toward others, are those conditions. The basic rights of others are due them because of their moral nature, because they have moral tasks in life that they must fulfill. Intruding on their sphere of moral jurisdiction amounts to thwarting their moral agency. And basic rights spell out where the conduct of others would or would not amount to intrusion. That is why the "border" analogy is useful, even if it runs the risk of giving too materialist an image of a person's sphere of moral authority. Moral agents require borders around them so as to know what their responsibilities are and where others must ultimately leave decisions up to them.

If Sam has a sphere of moral authority, and that sphere is indeed respected and protected, it will be Sam's task to do what is right and abstain from doing what is wrong in his life. For example, if Sam has a moral responsibility to develop his artistic talents, it needs to be left up to Sam whether to do so or not. If Judy were to force Sam to enter art school, say, by threatening to harm him, even if Sam were to become a successful artist, Sam could not take credit for the decision to pursue art. It might seem that Judy could take credit for Sam's enrollment, although Sam, not she, became the great artist. It is, first of all, wrong for Judy to thwart Sam's chances of doing the morally right act (even though Judy also prevented Sam from losing such credit and gaining blame for a bad decision). Judy's basic moral responsibility toward Sam—a person to whom Judy is not bound by other moral considerations, such as a contractual or parental obligation—is to refrain from intruding on him.

Sam has basic rights to life, liberty, and property, and it would be wrong for Judy to violate or abridge those rights, even if Judy had a correct view of the objectives Sam should pursue. It is a denial of Sam's moral agency by Judy, an assault on his dignity as a human being and moral agent, to substitute Judy's decision for Sam's in those kinds of matters. Of course, there can be many ways for Sam to benefit from Judy. But here, again, whether Judy will impart benefits or not is a matter for Judy to decide, even if it is evident enough to others that Judy ought to impart them. Sam has no right to such benefits, only to Judy's abstaining from intruding upon him.

There is much more that could be said about basic rights, but I have discussed the topic at much greater length elsewhere.[11] Suffice it to add that no more than the requirement to observe the negative individual human rights may be forced upon strangers as they relate to each other. That is because the rest of what they should do lies within their own moral jurisdictions. It pertains to them, to their own moral space, whereas respect of everyone's negative rights is required for the equal, mutually nonconflicting preservation of the moral agency and the requisite moral space of everyone. And to avoid the problems that stem from the occasional recalcitrant individual, institutions to secure negative rights should be established— ergo, government. (The "should" here comes from the imperative that one ought to do what makes it possible for one to flourish as an individual human being. To be prudent about the debilitating harm others can do to one is a clear example of a kind of virtue, namely, prudent conduct. So government as a protector of negative rights is the product of prudence, even though it serves to secure and administer justice.)

Rights and Generosity

How does all this apply to our topic, generosity? We must note, first of all, how respect for rights is not in the same moral category as the practice of virtues. When another is owed something by right, granting what is owed is not a matter of generosity, not a matter of practicing one of several virtues. It is not that kind of good deed but another, namely, respect without conditions for the other as a person.

When one acts without violation of other people's rights, there are several options. One may discover that to be generous is not the best option—not the most rational way to act under the circumstances. Instead, one should be prudent or tolerant or courageous or honest—or, again, some proper combination of all of those. Within the hierarchy of the virtues, one or another may dominate in any specific situation. When it comes to treating others simply as human beings who are fellow members of political communities—which is what is spelled out by reference to their fundamental rights as human beings—there is no such hierarchy. In other words, basic human rights are political imperatives to fully respect the sovereignty of all adult members of one's human community, so there is no option as to which of those rights need to be protected most vigilantly. This is where the issue of compossibility, including mutual respectability and protectability, comes in. For them all to be such, they must form a compossible set.

The idea of the indivisibility of human liberty addresses this point in the familiar political rhetoric of Americans. When in the Declaration of Independence all men are said to be equal, it is this point that is being made: no one's rights are more or less important than those of others, and all the basic rights are in need of being secured by government. That kind of equality is not about equal economic, educational, or medical conditions, the fair distribution to everyone of various goods and services others produce.

Human beings are equal in their possession of basic rights because they are all moral agents with responsibilities they must fulfill on their own initiative. In other matters it is clear enough that they are anything but equal—in how beautiful, healthy, talented, or fortunate they are.

At least vis-à-vis the fundamental rights of individual human beings, what one has the responsibility to do—namely, to respect everyone's basic rights—is *always* obligatory, regardless of circumstances.[12] (The only exception may be the situation that Locke is reported to have designated as one wherein "peace is not possible," that is, in extreme natural circumstances such as an earthquake or a famine.[13] The normal conditions within which human cooperation and coexistence may be reasonably expected are missing in these circumstances. That accounts for why courts tend to pardon many criminal transgressions when they occur in such circumstances.) Of course, respect for rights is not something entirely without moral content, and one may become habituated to respecting others' rights.

40

Yet, as already noted, someone who is so habituated is not acting generously but, more likely, is simply scrupulous, acting with ordinary attention to the standards of social and political propriety.

Put generally, generosity requires a kind of community life in which one's sovereignty is acknowledged—that is, where individuals have jurisdiction over themselves and their belongings. Of course, individual sovereignty does not have to be officially acknowledged, so long as it does receive some recognition by oneself and one's fellows, explicitly or even tacitly. (That is why, even in collectivist societies, people will be able to distinguish generous, courageous, and prudent conduct and individuals, even though that is rendered more difficult by the attempt to abolish privacy, the sphere wherein moral decisions are initiated. In short, the law denies but reality reaffirms the sphere of individual moral responsibility.) The point is that moral sovereignty[14] must be a fact taken to be such by the relevant parties—those who could act on or in defiance of it. As David Levine puts it, "When I have a right over some object or activity, this means that I determine the activity and the manner of the object's disposal. In this sense, my right endows me with power."[15] That power is what renders me an effective moral agent whose conduct can be right or wrong, depending on how the right is exercised (i.e., how the power is deployed).[16]

Now, if moral sovereignty were impossible for us, we would be unable to practice any virtue, least of all generosity. We would then probably be related to our society and to humanity as a whole in the way our arms and eyes are related to us, not as individuals with moral responsibilities of our own. Or we would be like the lower animals, like lobsters, that are not collectivist but cannibalistic. We could possess no moral virtues at all, since morality can exist only where the possibility of and the capacity for making some choices are present. One does not praise one's arm for a good discus throw, except figuratively. One's eyes are not given moral credit for having correctly detected disease, even if the eyes played a role in that detection. In short, if we were part of a collective whole, we could not be regarded as moral agents and our good traits could not be moral virtues.

Let us consider a person who is not a sovereign but who *belongs* to a tribe, community, or state.[17] He has nothing of his own to give or contribute for the benefit of another. If we were simply elements

41

of a larger whole—as is arguably advanced in Marx's understanding of communism—or elements of the "organic body" of humanity, there would be no opportunity for any of us to choose to give or to cultivate a giving character. We would have nothing of our own, and we would have no personal jurisdiction.

Generosity and Denying Individual Rights

In many communities the sovereignty of the individual is denied and the solidarity of the large organic body of the community is affirmed. If that were rigorously upheld, virtuous conduct, including generosity, would be impossible. Morally virtuous conduct, including generosity, is an option only for those who have their personal moral agency and sovereignty respected, whether explicitly or merely de facto. Thus, even in a collectivized kibbutz where people actually treat one another as sovereign members, there can be generosity (apart from de jure sharing).

Of course, since every individual is morally sovereign, the issue can only be whether that fact is acknowledged. Even where it is officially or doctrinally denied, a good measure of virtuous conduct will be evident. That is because many people in the community understand that they are indeed moral agents, individuals with personal moral tasks they can either accomplish or neglect. So even in a system where individual choices are disregarded and the moral sovereignty of every human individual is officially denied, there will be evidence of such sovereignty in the lives of numerous individuals.

Of course, official denial does often manage to obscure facts. In many societies the individual's sovereignty has been and is being denied. In earlier times that was nearly universal, and even in ours there is ample evidence of such denial around the globe. But at the same time, defiance of that denial is also rampant.

A number of philosophers argue that the moral sovereignty of individual human beings—the requirement that each make those choices that determine whether the agent will do the right or the wrong thing—is an invention, not a discovery of a fact about human beings. That group may or may not include people who simply deny the reality of free will—that one has the capacity, normally, to initiate one's conduct, which could turn out well or badly. Of those there are many, and their view, too, seriously undercuts public acknowledgment of moral sovereignty and responsibility.[18]

The historicist objection to individualism has significant implications for our understanding of a virtue such as generosity. If indeed there have been eras in which human beings were properly regarded as not morally sovereign—say, in those in which, maybe quite properly, their will had to be[19] subjugated to the tribe, clan, family, race, or whatever (because, say, of the absolute necessity of such subjugation for mere survival)—then those people could not be said to be responsible for cultivating the virtue of generosity—or any other virtue, for that matter. As individuals, none—except perhaps a leader—could be held responsible for doing anything, including the right thing or the cultivation of a right attitude that would prompt one to do the right thing.

We have already noted, of course, that such absence of individual sovereignty also involves the absence of individual rights. As Auguste Comte (who coined the term "altruism") noted, the

> social point of view . . . cannot tolerate the notion of rights, for such a notion rests on individualism. We are born under a load of obligations of every kind, to our predecessors, to our successors, to our contemporaries. After our birth those obligations increase or accumulate, for it is some time before we can return any service. . . . This ["to live for others"], the definitive formula of human morality, gives a direct sanction exclusively to our instincts of benevolence, the common source of happiness and duty. [Man must serve] Humanity, whose we are entirely.[20]

That position, while it shares the tenor of much of contemporary moral and, especially, social and political philosophy, is nevertheless in contradiction to the ethics of virtue and to the moral point of view. A morally significant course must be a chosen course. If the "agent" belongs to some tribe, state, or community, or humanity at large, as Comte would have it, there is no room left for individual moral choice. All behavior occurs on behalf of the whole and requires the will of the whole. Individual moral responsibility is eradicated in the process.[21] For example, those who champion communitarianism would be hard-pressed to contend that, for example, Ghanaians ought to revise their practice of subjecting 10-year-old virgins to slavery under guise of having them atone for their parents' or other family members' sins since, as the *New York Times* reported, they "say the practice stems from a world view that sees justice and

43

punishment in communal rather than individual terms; an individual who has no connection to a crime may be punished to spare others."[22]

Moral virtues are a chosen, not coerced, disposition to practice principles of morality, especially when we are talking about the conduct of adults. Generosity, as a virtue, cannot exist unless there exists a significant degree of moral sovereignty, the condition that renders choice possible for moral agents.

In Chapter 5, I will address a particularly interesting and influential argument against the position defended above. That will be done in connection with the idea that some exchanges, for example, trading one's blood for cash, should be legally banned, "blocked." For the time being, however, let us just keep in mind the idea that virtues are morally significant only if vices are also possible.

3. Institutional Generosity

Remote Generosity

In complex social circumstances, men and women will not engage in generous conduct the same way they would in simple social settings. When people who know each other or share goals and values live scattered about the country, connected by complicated technology, generous acts will differ from those in a medieval village or an ancient Greek polis. Giving some seed to a neighboring farmer in times of bad harvest, being a midwife to a woman who is giving birth to a child, and helping a family rebuild a burned-out home could be generous acts. But is it, in the late 20th century, a generous act to send by way of one's modem a copy of the phone numbers of prospective customers to a fellow merchant just embarking upon a new venture?

It is not only technology that raises such questions. Institutional generosity emerges as a process of trust between like-minded persons interested in promoting ends that are of mutual value. Philanthropy is one result. Learning that there are deserving persons with whom one shares an interest in some political, artistic, literary, ecological, or athletic cause, one might elect to choose an intermediary to disburse some valued help. Contributing to a wildlife fund that will enable experts to perform most effectively may be an example of indirect, institutional generosity.

Such institutionalized generosity is not new; it is thousands of years old—the burial societies of ancient times and the mediaeval *Stiftungen*, monasteries, fraternal orders, and the like all qualify. Does that fact contradict the earlier assertions about the nondeliberative, spontaneous character of generosity? Surely writing out a check each month and mailing it to some organization would seem to be both deliberate and impersonal. Yet the actual decision to give to either an intimate or a remote beneficiary could well be spontaneous, the result of one's "second nature" to be alert to opportunities that call forth one's help and support. And the knowledge that one shares values with another person who is spatially remote and otherwise

45

unfamiliar to one would make one's involvement with the other personal, would distinguish that person from strangers whose values and goals one does not know.

People make generous gifts to the Nature Conservancy and the Promise Keepers. Sometimes gifts are a matter of one's sense of obligation or duty to those organizations; one may believe that one owes some support to such a group as a matter of some moral duty. In that case, the giving would be generous only if it went beyond what is a recognizable expectation of the fulfillment of this obligation. That is when we can reasonably speak of a generous contribution, for clearly, not all contributions are generous; some involve only a token amount or "whatever is expected," while others are generous. Still, the main point here is that one can be generous to or through an institution as well as directly to people one knows intimately. And generosity will not thereby lose its property of being a virtue. What makes it an authentic moral virtue is that the decision to give, the sense that giving is the right thing to do, is itself produced not by deliberation but by a cultivated inclination or habit.

Limits on Institutional Generosity

There are limits to how far one can be generous through institutions. In each case, there must be some spontaneous affinity that generates the generous act. Otherwise the act will be one not so much of generosity as of duty or obligation. When a donor to a foundation sends off an especially large check or puts up an especially dear item for auction in a fundraising effort, that act must spring from a well-ingrained sense of the worth of the beneficiary's works, not be in consequence of a debt owed, for it to amount to an act of generosity. Those who will be enabled to do their work better as a result cannot simply expect or claim a right to the contribution.

When such contributions are numerous enough and have a history, especially within a large community, they can, of course, generate support for ongoing work, including assistance aimed at helping needy persons, advancing worthy projects that must be carried out over some period of time to bear fruit, and assisting organizations to stand ready to repair damage from natural disasters. (For example, a generous person may incline toward helping those who are harmed by California earthquakes or North Dakota floods, as well as by the

46

farther removed catastrophes around the globe. Though those are not regularly occurring events, they can be expected to occur now and then and cause major disruptions in the lives of thousands of people.)

The origin of such generous conduct would be some generous impulse, perhaps arising from learning about some disaster and how innocent people have been hurt by it, or from reading a work of fiction that calls to mind such events. One may, for example, have seen the film *Schindler's List*, and its impact may be to call forth a sense of longing to reach out to survivors of the Holocaust, who may have been some of the children the Nazis treated with such callousness and hatred and whose lives one can imagine are quite a struggle. A generous soul, with the requisite means, may well be moved to send off a check, even pledge a monthly contribution over the foreseeable future, in consequence of such a feeling. That generosity would be directed, normally, only to the remaining few who have not yet recovered from the aftereffects of the horrific event. The beneficiaries might also be victims of other but similar cruelties, say, in Bosnia or Rwanda.

Or a social scientist with a generous disposition might respond by dedicating himself to some study that could shed some light on how anti-Semitism can best be detected and dealt with in the schools or elsewhere in a culture. Even an author of popular novels might respond to such an event—or to any other source of generous feelings—with a resolution to craft a work of fiction that could dramatize the evil of such horrors and how decent people might go about coping with it.[1]

The central notable fact here is that the virtue of generosity, while spontaneous in the sense of functioning as a character trait rather than a conclusion to intellectual deliberation (as, say, a duty would), can produce results that may become standard features of a community. In short, generosity itself may appear to have become institutionalized. Yet in fact, it is certain organizational requirements, not changes in generosity itself, that are involved in such institutionalization.

So, charitable or philanthropic organizations have certain attributes that reflect the spontaneous nature of the virtue of generosity. For one thing, they cannot guarantee support; they can promise to help only to the extent of the generosity of members of the relevant community. Furthermore, those administering the organizations will need to send out reminders, when that is reasonable, so that generous people will have occasion to give their generosity active expression. The contemporary phenomenon of mass mailings from the American Red Cross, AmeriCare, United Way, and other agencies attempting to satisfy various more or less urgent needs and aspirations illustrates this point.

There is another limitation derived from the necessarily voluntary nature of generosity. Institutional generosity would have to be part of the private sector in any society, instead of an entitlement program of a welfare state. In somewhat starker terms, there is nothing generous about the U.S. Congress or the California state legislature appropriating—or is it *ex*propriating?—funds for those who have suffered injuries or property damage from a flood or earthquake.

Relief for AIDS patients cannot be considered a result of generosity if those whose resources make it possible do not voluntarily provide their support. And even though it is often said that the American people are very generous in the appropriation of tax revenues to send to foreign lands, this cannot be right except in a perverse sense, namely, that the public as a whole—that is, the majority of politically active Americans—does not take action to counter state policies of wealth redistribution in the form of foreign aid. The government— that is, those currently occupying the various positions where public policies are forged—cannot properly be considered generous, since the funds appropriated and supposedly distributed to deserving needy parties do not belong to those giving them away.

Such notions of government "generosity" are implied by certain theories developed fully only in the 20th century. Among them we find the view that those to whom governments provide benefits— welfare payments, subsidies, foreign aid, price supports, grants, and so forth—actually have the basic right to receive them.[2] According to that line of thinking, providing and obtaining such benefits is a matter not of generosity but of justice. In some sense, the benefits actually belong to those who receive them, and all that governments do is transfer funds from those who happen to hold them to those who actually own them. And the appropriate response of recipients is not gratitude but, at most, acknowledgment of respectful treatment. If such treatment is, however, not forthcoming, the proper response is not a plea or moral exhortation but litigation or political action.

48

We may conclude, then, that institutional generosity is not a defining feature of a welfare state, contrary to the impression created by talk of "the people's" compassion or generosity toward the needy in their society. Only when the crucial element of voluntariness is present, as in the establishment and administration of philanthropic or similar care-providing organizations, can we properly assess the parties involved in providing the support as practicing the virtue of generosity. Moral credit cannot properly be given to those whose behavior conforms to morality unintentionally or involuntarily (as in involuntary servitude).

Nor can it be that generous support of charitable work is something the donor is dutybound to provide, as in the case of being legally required to repay a debt. Instead, the donor must see the work and the people performing it in a friendly light—the donor must feel some affinity with them that leads him to extend himself in their direction beyond the call of duty.

Shame and Generosity

Any particular instance of not extending oneself in that way does not properly make one feel moral guilt, either. If guilt is warranted, it is on occasions when one comes to the realization, over time, that one lacks generosity and as a result comes to feel a sense of moral failing in life. But such shame at not living up to the requirements of virtue is not the same as guilt due to some breach of duty or obligation.

Suppose one has just received a solicitation for funds or some other contribution—possibly the donation of some of one's spare time and skills—for a cause whose worth one abstractly but clearly acknowledges. On such an occasion, if one is not able to honor the request, the decision to withhold support may result in some sadness or regret, but not guilt. One may regret not being able to do what one thinks might be a worthy thing—supporting a good cause or those who strive to achieve it. But if one were, in fact, dutybound to make a contribution—perhaps to an organization that stands for one's basic convictions, to the extremely needy in one's community, or to the treasury of one's political party (which supposedly is advancing what one believes is a vital cause)—not doing so would probably bring on feelings of guilt.

It is different with occasions for generosity. If one had been ungenerous and realized—say, in some moment of self-scrutiny—that one had become hardened to the call for help and consistently failed to further what is clearly of value to one, then a sense of shame would be appropriate. Such hardening would be a matter of a defect or defects in one's character. The realization of it could even manifest itself in a deep blush.

That reckoning, incidentally, is no guarantee that the person will begin to reform his character. Interpretation of one's emotional response to moral failure need not be accurate and may easily be influenced by motives of self-vindication and evasion of responsibility. Yet when we combine the element of shame with the social repercussions and general untoward results experienced by guilty parties, the likelihood of adjustment in behavior increases, because continued stinginess will be disadvantageous. For example, one hears a great deal of lamentation about the alleged failure of the state to care for the needy. Were the virtue of generosity talked up, instead, by those voices in society that usually promulgate moral ideals—religious leaders, fiction writers, celebrities, politicians, talk show hosts—this could well contribute to a better cultural atmosphere. In the resulting climate of opinion generosity would be encouraged instead of neglected.

The "Generous" Commonwealth

Strictly speaking, only individuals can choose to be morally virtuous, including generous. It may, however, make sense to speak of a generous community, corporation, or family, provided it is kept in mind that such generosity comes from the persons who make up the groups in question. This is no different from the realization that when we speak of the Soviet invasion of Hungary, we in fact have in mind the thousands of Soviet soldiers, their officers, and ultimately the Soviet dictatorship's leaders.

In line with such an outlook, if the moral sovereignty of human individuals did not exist, generosity would not be possible. Of course, a kind of replacement might manifest itself in rebellion against the general social structure, as when under communism someone must courageously break the rule of communal ownership. (As Robert Heilbroner so perceptively notes,[3] under communism everyone's labor belongs to the community as a whole, so even lending another a hand could strictly be considered impermissible—one would require the permission of the community, so only the community as a whole might conceivably be considered generous, never an individual.)

Even in voluntary communes, special benevolent outreach toward one person might be viewed with suspicion since it might tend to undermine the disciplined prior obligation of all to the whole. Of course, many groups lack a precise form, so people treat each other in mixed fashion—as friends, compatriots, associates, neighbors, and so forth—and there are numerous moral dimensions that can be manifest, some of which appear to contradict the others. A family is a communal arrangement, but generosity is clearly possible between its members.

In any case, whatever the merits of the kind of communal living in which members are treated as belonging to the whole unit, generosity is unlikely to be a virtue under such a system. It is incompatible with any kind of actual, strictly maintained collectivism—that is, a system under which the sovereignty of the individual is effectively rejected in favor of total or substantial subservience to some common purpose—whether freely accepted or imposed, except, perhaps, if the initial choice to join such a collective is itself motivated by generosity.

Without effective individual sovereignty, there would be nothing about which one could make a decision. And that would preclude most virtues, since they all presuppose the moral initiative of the individual person who possesses or lacks them. No room would be left for generosity—the choice to benefit others with one's skills or belongings, or with anything else of one's own. The decision to join a collective farm may, however, involve the generous contribution of one's skills. However, in the opinions of some thinkers, as noted above, one does not even own those and the decision to devote them to some task or another must be left to the collective and not to oneself.

Both direct, personal generosity and indirect, institutional generosity presuppose human communities in which a significant degree of personal sovereignty exists. Such communities would also have to include a significant degree of respect for a system of stable private-property rights, and that system would have to be extensive enough to permit the development of habits of ownership of valued skills, items, time, and so forth on the part of individuals. Only with such a stable system of private-property rights can generosity be expected to be a part of the character of members of the community. Without such a system, lack of generosity generates not so much particularized guilt as lack of self-esteem on the part of those who are not allowed to be generous.

4. Generosity via Government?

Integrity and Generosity

Rights and enforceable obligations are correlative; if one has the right to be free from other people's intrusive conduct, others have the obligation, which can be enforced by the one with the right or by authorized agents, to not engage in such conduct. If, in turn, one has the right to be provided with help from others, then others are again obligated to provide that help and may be forced to do so.[1] Those who demand that "generosity," "charity," "compassion," or "kindness" be legally secured by coercive governments—welfare statists, socialists, and to some extent communitarians—actually destroy the foundation of those moral virtues, by changing them from virtues into enforceable duties. They render the conduct something the agent cannot choose freely, without being coerced. Despite all the rhetoric about compassion, kindness, and charity, supporters of the welfare state in effect make it impossible for citizens to be compassionate, kind, and charitable. They advocate the demoralization of society.

In the following pages we will examine the relationship of generosity to political society. It has already been observed that the flourishing of the virtuous life, including generosity, requires widespread respect for and protection of certain political principles. To conduct oneself as a morally virtuous person, a human being must enjoy the protection of certain basic rights—to life, liberty, and property—and related, more specialized rights. Personal responsibility for acting generously, honestly, prudently, courageously, and so forth would not be possible if one were simply a limb on, or a cell in, the body of the organic whole of a tribe, nation, ethnic group, or any sort of community (as often supposed by various collectivist social thinkers and visionaries).

The sort of individualism presupposed in the ethics of virtue is not "atomistic individualism," the view that human beings are self-sufficient apart from society. Interdependence among human beings, based on innumerable, often disparate factors, is a fact of life to be heeded—by the cultivation of such virtues as generosity, liberality, tolerance, fraternity, loyalty, and so on. Nevertheless, the virtuous human life does presuppose, for its very possibility, some measure of decisiveness on the part of individual humans regarding what they will do in life, including what communities they will join, avoid, or associate with only in part.

Critics of individualism claim that any theory of individual rights rests on atomism. It is most unfortunate that in the critiques of individualism no attempt is made to discover a more generous rendition of this social philosophy, one that sees the high regard individualism has for the individual human as a locus of moral virtue, as a being capable of making choices that merit praise or blame.[2]

Instead, we find the critics presenting a version of individualism some aspects of which are obviously morally repugnant and often wholly unrealistic. Individualists are presented as holding that all human beings are isolated, atomistic creatures whose "independence" is not the virtue of trying, for example, to ascertain truth and justice objectively, without prejudice and free of group pressure, but the vice of fantasizing some kind of solitary existence, of denying moral connections and responsibilities to family and friends, espousing hedonism or reckless self-indulgence and greed as either an innate drive or something socially necessary. The fact that most individualists, qua social and political theorists, are in fact mainly concerned with showing the unjustifiability of interpersonal oppression and thus denying a natural subservience of any human being to some supposedly higher group—which is most often translated as subservience to some select other persons—does not appear to pacify the critics. It is difficult to appreciate their concerns when they see such a goal as so lacking in any merit.

A good example of that approach may be found in Charles Taylor's essay "Atomism."[3] Here Taylor claims that the classical-liberal polity (wherein the protection of basic negative rights is the primary public policy) necessarily presupposes what he calls atomism. He links this view to Hobbes and Locke.

> Theories which assert the primacy of rights are those which take as the fundamental, or at least a fundamental, principle of their political theory the ascription of certain rights to individuals and which deny the same status to a principle of belonging or obligation, that is a principle which states

54

our obligation as men to belong to or sustain society, or a
society of a certain type, or to obey authority or an authority
of a certain type.[4]

Actually, there are theories of individual rights that begin with
the moral responsibility to find self-fulfillment in the company of
other people in society, even if not with a strong and perhaps enforceable duty to belong to any specified society. Contrary to Taylor's
claim, even Locke hints at such moral responsibilities.

> The state of nature has a law of nature to govern it, which
> obliges every one: and reason, which is that law, teaches all
> mankind, who will but consult it, that being all equal and
> independent, no one ought to harm another in his life, health,
> liberty or possessions.[5]

Since he is primarily concerned in his *Two Treatises of Government*
with politics, the laws of nature of concern to him involve the guid-
ance of community life. Here natural rights are significant. But Locke
does not preclude other laws of nature—for example, "reason, which
is that law." That Locke focuses on the teaching of reason about
how we ought to act toward each other has to do with his specific
project, namely, identifying the principles of political life. He also
states that

> every one, as he is bound to preserve himself, and not to
> quit his station willfully, so by the like reason when his own
> preservation comes not in competition, ought he, as much
> as he can, to preserve the rest of mankind, and may not,
> unless it be to do justice to an offender, take away or impair
> the life, or what tends to the preservation of life, the liberty,
> health, limb, or goods of another.[6]

So, the moral responsibility to preserve oneself or to be generous
could well be another of the natural principles of social life. Arguably
for Locke, then, prior to the *right* to life, which is a political principle,
there exists the ethical obligation or responsibility to preserve one's
life—in other words, the moral virtue of self-interest. The law of
nature obliges us all to abstain from harming others. According to
Locke's understanding of natural rights, this law implies the rights
to one's person and estate. It does not mean, however, that rights
are fundamental rather than based on prior moral responsibilities.

So Taylor is wrong to hold so confidently that Locke *begins* his understanding of politics with individual rights (even if he is correct to say that Hobbes does, albeit with an understanding of rights very different from Locke's). Locke begins with laws of nature and then proceeds to concentrate on that law or principle of morality that requires respect for others' natural rights.

In the state of nature, there are obligations. Some of them, such as not to kill or rob another, rest on natural rights and are enforceable: "No one ought to harm another in his life, health, liberty or possessions." But Locke does not preclude other moral imperatives that have to do with our relationship to others, as well as with how we act vis-à-vis our own lives. It looks very much like Locke believed that we ought to consult our reason, to discover the various laws of nature by which we ought to live our lives, and that we ought to preserve ourselves and, "when his own preservation comes not in competition . . . the rest of mankind."

The obligation not to violate others' natural rights, which Locke thinks we are *justified* in enforcing, even when we aren't powerful enough to do so, is, however, too weak a statement of political duty for those who, like Taylor, want us to *belong* to society, to be society's possessions.[7] Lockean negative rights require that no one place another under his or her will or power.

Taylor wants to usher in positive rights—*rights to be provided for by all those who belong and are thus obligated to make provisions.* Individualists think, however, that we have and may enforce only negative obligations—to abstain from harming other people in their lives, health, liberty, or possessions. And if those obligations are not fulfilled, they may be enforced—by the establishment of a government, for instance.

Nothing in this view precludes the serious nonlegal or ethical obligations people have in society—loved ones to each other, brothers to brothers, friends to friends, colleagues to colleagues, and so forth. But because we are by nature free and independent, we are forbidden to assume mastery over other people: in Locke's words, "There cannot be supposed any such subordination among us that may authorize us to destroy one another, as if we were made for one another's uses, as the inferior ranks of creatures are for ours."[8]

Taylor laments that, in part because he thinks our choices are not always mature enough to guide us toward self-fulfillment.[9] He even invokes the idea of false consciousness (also found in Marx's account of "capitalist" society) to indicate when people are not qualified to be free in the Lockean sense.[10] But an individualist would say that (a) the initial stages of self-development are the task of parents, next of kin, neighbors, and friends of the family, not of the state, whose sole role in our lives is to guard our rights in society and (b) ordinarily, each of us (except for the very unfortunate, for whom special provisions, such as a guardian-ward relationship, can be made) will be able to set ourselves to the task of self-development, with help, when necessary, from society, not the state.

Taylor also claims that before Hobbes and Locke there was no reference to individual rights, which is flatly contradicted by the evidence.[11] Perhaps all that Taylor means is just what the Lockean tradition affirms: we have ethical obligations apart from anything just laws would require of us. But surely this isn't what Taylor wishes to stress, despite his use of the term "obligation." Are we to understand "obligation" as a course of conduct that is mandatory and enforceable, or a matter of moral requirement? If it is *morally* required, one then needs to be free from the coercive interventions of others if one is to fulfill the obligation or to do what one ought morally to do, no matter that some people may often be unwilling to do so. Lack of resoluteness is no excuse—it is, indeed, a moral failing but not one that may be remedied by coercive measures. If the "obligation" is mandatory, others may impose it upon one by force. But then no moral credit for good behavior is due the one who fulfills the obligation; the most that is due is a recognition that the individual has fulfilled the requirements for civilized community life—has upheld standards of justice.[12] In contrast, a morally virtuous life includes recognition that human nature requires extensive social engagement, as well as acting on this fact, but it does not require that such engagement be unconditional.[13]

Perhaps the ambiguity in Taylor can be removed by noting that he equates a principle of obligation with a principle of belonging. Yet it is possible to understand moral virtues that are not legal obligations with correlative rights, as well as legal obligations that do not entail any further legal or moral relationships. For example, one may be morally obliged to be generous or kind or helpful without its being true that one may be forced to act accordingly. Similarly, my legal obligation to repay a debt need not imply any other, more extensive, legal relationships. I pay my debts to foreigners, for example, despite having no other legal or political relationships with them.

But for Taylor, being obligated means *belonging* to the object of such an obligation. That has rather ominous implications, for it is slaves who belong and do service, not from their sense of morality or ethics, but from the requirement to comply with the demands of whomever they belong to.[14]

In contrast, when men and women—moral agents who possess both free will and moral responsibilities—act virtuously, it is because they choose to do so. Taylor completely ignores this distinction between an enforceable (legal) and an unenforceable (ethical) obligation. Because of that he never has to deal with whether the social nature of human beings is something they need to fulfill as a matter of their moral responsibilities, or something they can be forced to fulfill at the power-backed commands of others.

Overstating Individualism

It is important for critics of individualism to consider, not only how wildly certain elements of our nature might be exaggerated in some accounts, but also how exaggerating aspects of our nature in one way may be far more harmful than doing so in another. Thus, while it is true that individualism can be propounded in an arid fashion, such as in some economists' approach to understanding human life, that has been far less harmful than the similarly exaggerated rosy collectivist accounts.

Surely one concern in an evaluation of alternative social systems ought to be to consider how corruptible respective systems can be. And collectivism certainly has fared badly in some of its renditions if we judge by simple common sense—something we ignore at our peril in the midst of trying to tie everything to some theory.

Ethnic, religious, tribal, national, economic, and other human groupings have wreaked havoc aplenty upon humanity throughout history. The Nazi horrors, ethnic cleansings, mob lynchings, the Inquisition, and the like all provide examples of collectivism having gone awry to various degrees. Consider, as just one example, the Russian author Tatyana Tolstaya's observation, in an essay written for the *New Republic* shortly after the fall of the Soviet Union, of the nature of one grand horrid example of collectivist social organization.

> According to [collectivists] "the people" is a living organism,
> not a "mere mechanical conglomeration of disparate individ-
> uals." This, of course, is the old, inevitable trick of totalitarian
> thinking: "the people" is posited as unified and whole in its
> multiplicity. It is a sphere, a swarm, an anthill, a beehive, a
> body. And a body should strive for perfection; everything
> in it should be smooth, sleek, and harmonious. Every organ
> should have its place and its function: the heart and brain
> are more important than the nails and the hair, and so on.
> If your eye tempts you, then tear it out and throw it away;
> cut off sickly members, curb those limbs that will not obey,
> and fortify your spirit with abstinence and prayer.[15]

Tolstaya's choice of terms may suggest to some that this is clearly an overstatement of the collectivist position. But is it really an exaggeration? Marx himself refers to human society as "an organic body."[16] We have already seen that "belong" is Taylor's preferred term. What else does that suggest but the idea that human beings are components of some larger body and are, thus, ultimately not self-directed? Indeed, it means that some persons or person—a majority, a politburo, a central committee, a dictator—will direct everyone's life, not that the whole body will do so in some cohesive, integrated fashion.

In contrast, the worst that can be said about individualism is that even in its most arid rendition, and when practiced apart from any consideration of human sociality—for example, in the context of highly calculative economic affairs—individuals are not relating to one another in personable ways, kindly and compassionately. They clearly often objectify one another: the butcher, baker, and candle-stick maker are treated primarily as instruments of one's purpose. Yet even here such instrumentality is predicated on people's choices, on their willingness, under certain circumstances, to cooperate as instruments of each other's ends. Taken too far, this can be alienating, indeed, but who says one has to take it too far?

Periodically, one may have to focus nearly exclusively on business, so parenting and friendship and generosity need to be set aside (e.g., when there are upheavals in the marketplace or nature has dealt a blow to one's enterprise). But there is no necessity to maintain that focus. One can recover a more balanced approach to living. One is not regimented into some condition of helpless subservience, as one surely is when the collectivist alternative goes awry.

In an attempt to understand human ideals, it is not enough to pick the best conceivable rendition of what a given ideal might bring forth. In the case of Marx, that would amount to thinking of humanity as a seamless whole that lives in total internal harmony, a "species being," with no part pitted against any other—rather like a high-caliber orchestra or a beehive at its best. (There clearly are examples of human groups that behave in such a fashion, and there is something wonderful about that—as when an acrobatic team shows itself to be fully coordinated—but it is hard to imagine that as providing a kind of general social ideal.)

Individualism, properly and charitably understood, amounts to the view that human beings are by nature the sort of living beings whose flourishing requires self-directed, creative rational thought and conduct. They possess the fundamental attributes of the capacity and need for autonomy and moral responsibility. They are indeed social animals, yet their sociality is to be understood as involving critical selections from among alternative social arrangements (at least once they reach adulthood). The fact that at some times and places throughout human history individuality has been suppressed is not evidence of the nonessentiality of individuality. It is evidence, instead, of the ill-conceived social circumstances under which too many human beings have had to live throughout history or of some people's willingness to subjugate themselves, to accept a subservient role in the governance of their lives.

To put it succinctly, individualism stresses the fundamentality of human moral agency in the life of every human being. By this account, the morally virtuous life requires a substantial element of individualism in how people in a culture understand themselves and their social-political institutions.

Virtuous generosity, too, requires support from a political system that does not usurp personal virtue. We have already noted that this implies that the neglect of generosity by someone would have to be politically but not morally tolerated; it is being generous to a fault to ignore unexplained lack of generosity in many others. A liberal social order that recognizes individual sovereignty is most conducive to generosity. Of course, this is but a particular implication of the more general point that in such a society, personal virtues are left to individual initiative rather than to legislation.

But is it reasonable to focus exclusively on personal virtue when discussing the possible generosity of a community? We have already noted that there is ample room for institutional generosity in a good human community. Firms, clubs, churches, schools, and other groups may institute more or less generous policies in the appropriate spheres of their operations. Why not, it might be asked, extend this possibility to government?

There is at least one crucial reason why such extension might not be appropriate, although we cannot explore here whether it is decisive: there is a serious danger to the integrity of a legal administration if its administrators yield to considerations of generosity in carrying out their duties.

A useful analogy would be the way a referee or judge behaves at an athletic event. When judging a diving competition or refereeing a tennis tournament, those who are entrusted with the responsibility for judging correctly and faithfully—that is, by strict adherence to the standards—have no option to interject some other consideration, such as generosity or kindness. The integrity of the role demands that only what is called for from the position held—judge, referee, umpire—be taken as a guide to conduct. The same may be said of the role of teachers as graders, the role of parents as fair-minded adjudicators of sibling disputes, and so forth.

Generosity versus Fairness

Of course, if someone in an athletic contest were hurt, a referee who had first-aid skills might offer help. That could be a generous act that would in no way compromise the role of referee. When a doctor helps a patient in some issue unrelated to medicine, say, by providing financial advice or clues about where one might find the best real-estate agent in town, there is generosity, but it should not come at the expense of duty or professional responsibilities.

But if a referee simply notices what a player could do to advance his objectives, that does not justify abandoning the referee position or attempting to mix that position with that of a fan or a coach. Nor is it justified for a surgeon to leave an operation to help some other patient with some personal or even professional problem. Barring some peculiar circumstances, doing so would involve a serious breach of duty.

Similarly, when a police officer is asked for directions by a lost person, a helpful and courteous response, provided no duty is being

61

neglected or breached, would by no means involve anything inappropriate. And this gives us a clue as to the nature of generosity on the part of governments. The central issue is what governments are for. For a government, there is an especially crucial issue at stake if it extends itself in special ways toward some members of the public but not toward others. That is especially so if even a modicum of democratic theory of government is sound.

Fairness, in the sense of impartiality, is a vital virtue of governments, since these organizations are paid for by the entire membership of the community. Any special treatment would very likely imply using for some citizens resources that would be taken from all citizens, and raises the specter of group warfare, which is hardly compatible with generosity.

Consider, as a rather extreme case, deficit spending, a way to finance certain services for which no revenues have been raised. This may be deemed a generous thing to do. In fact, it is far from it. First, even if the revenues could be raised by way of taxes, the expenditures would not involve generosity since the resources do not belong to those who appropriate the funds. Furthermore, even if the framework of democratic public finance is fully accepted, support funded by debt that future generations will have to pay off involves breach of duty to those members of future generations who will have to repay the debt and yet have had no say about how to allocate what they will have to pay into the treasury.

Emergency and the Generosity of Governments

If the duty of impartiality is so central to good government, and if generosity consumes resources and extending it through government would generally involve favoring some citizens over others, would not all cases of government generosity involve some breach of duty? Not so. That is because, even for an agent of government, there are possibilities for extending oneself without breach of duty, as spontaneously as that is possible for an agent of a private institution. Let me put this differently: those individuals who are active in governmental service may find themselves at times faced with opportunities for generosity that can only be acted on in their capacity as civil servants, in light of the nature of the institution of government, including the powers that are available to it. It could be the case that although such powers ought to be used for specific, legally prescribed purposes, on rare occasions they could have uses that would amount to generous conduct.

This is where we find that a government can, as can any large institution with the requisite powers, enter the picture in times of far-reaching catastrophes such as earthquakes and floods when the resources of the private charitable institutions are stretched to their limits. But the government would enter, not as a matter of its primary obligation or job description, but rather as a gesture of goodwill toward persons in need of emergency services. (And provisions might be made in society that would render it superfluous for governments ever to leave their posts, as it were.) Just as a police officer would help an elderly person who has fallen down—though not, perhaps, if it were to interfere with his duty to stop a crime being committed on his beat—so a government could extend itself, temporarily, for purposes of assisting someone or some group in dire need.

The manner in which a government can be generous is by being, first, frugal and setting aside funds for emergencies without having to raise additional or special funds from citizens. A company, for example, can support the arts or education or community services by allocating some funds to those causes, provided they voluntarily receive funds for their products or services. If, for example, the legal, military, and police services of governments of free countries could be employed rapidly to forestall some disaster, without detracting from their primary purposes or displacing voluntary efforts, deploying them might be the proper thing to do. Officials of governments could, thus, embark on some generous deeds, not unlike officials of a corporation could, even while primarily concerned with fulfilling their obligation to increase their stockholders' returns on their investments. Corporate philanthropy may be generous without undercutting primary corporate purposes. Governments could be similarly generous.

Suffice it to note that some measure of institutional generosity is possible even from a government sworn to impartiality and equal protection of the law for all citizens, provided that does not compromise its integrity and does not provide an opportunity simply to expand state powers to "do good."

However, that would require a reshaping of most governments. Their purpose would have to be recognized as provision of legal justice and relevant services concerned with the protection and maintenance of legal justice, rather than the redistribution of the product of the work and savings of others. With that goal conscientiously pursued, there could be room for generosity as well, just as in each individual's life there can be room for generosity after the requirements of prudence and other prior virtues have been fulfilled.

No full elaboration and defense of the relationship between the virtue of generosity and the precise character of good government will be provided here. We have already seen what some of the essential ingredients of such a relationship amount to. Here it is necessary only to indicate how a conception of generosity as a significant human virtue would relate to a conception of a good political order that stands ready to preserve the conditions required for the development and exercise of that virtue.

Contrary to Thomas Nagel, as quoted in the Preface of this monograph, it is not "unreasonable to ask" that individuals "be generous when asked to give voluntarily." Nagel says that leaving generosity to individual initiative "is an excessively demanding moral position because it requires voluntary decisions that are quite difficult to make. Most people will tolerate a universal system of compulsory taxation without feeling entitled to complain, whereas they would feel justified in refusing an appeal that they contribute the same amount voluntarily."[17]

Actually, it is a mistake to think that something is excessively morally demanding "because it requires voluntary decisions that are quite difficult to make." Consider that it is quite difficult to make the decision to abstain from hitting someone who has insulted or offended, yet we do require that persons restrain themselves in the heat of anger, however difficult that may be. It is surely no excuse under the law that one's passions were inflamed, at least in most modern systems, and where such an excuse does carry the day, it is ultimately demeaning, an insult to the citizenry, who are treated by such an approach as children, not as adults who can and ought to exercise self-control. But perhaps that is not a good reply because, after all, to hit someone is against the law, so the resolve not to strike back isn't a moral but a legally induced one. However, there is ample evidence of moral resolve, as when folks keep promises they find a nuisance to honor, or remain faithful when tempted to betray, or embark upon difficult tasks that they would rather avoid. All the vices are tempting, yet often enough people resist them.

Furthermore, if the temptation to vice were so irresistible, one wonders why governments, composed not of angels or gods, would be such a safe bet. Trusting politicians and bureaucrats with the enormous powers entailed in paternalistic policies poses tremendous temptations to abuse them. That alone would warrant great restraint in the advocacy of government regulation of the conduct of citizens.

To expect adults to pay attention to and help alleviate the needs of deserving others, and to refrain from punishing them when they fall short, is to treat them as grown-ups.

It is paternalistic to believe that they have no such responsibility but may be forced to comply with laws that mandate the behavior that voluntary generous conduct would involve. Children are forced to be prudent; they are dragged to the dentist against their will because it is right for them to take care of their teeth, and *at their age,* fear of pain will stop them from doing what is right. It is demoralizing to apply the same rationale to forcing adults to do the right thing, including to be generous.

It also bears noting that Nagel has an idealized view of the taxation policies of the welfare state, at the same time that he has a cynical view of individual moral capacity. The taxation policies of the welfare state may well be rhetorically supported by reference to the needs of the poor and elderly, but in fact, they lead to countrywide squabbling about how the treasury's wealth will be redistributed among various interest groups. The poor—the folks who are in real need, who are helpless and destitute through no or only minimal fault of their own—usually have no capacity to make their claims forcefully in this squabble and are, thus, left out in the end. Yes, it usually begins with pleas for the poor and the elderly—especially, of course, the children of the poor—but in the last analysis, the process that is established to administer the welfare state fails the very folks who were used as the excuse to establish and maintain that system.

Furthermore, the necessity of a welfare program for some of the welfare state's most favored clients stands in serious dispute. As Norman Barry has noted,

> Although superficially it looks as if state provisions for the elderly is a perfect case of legitimate welfare activity by the state (historically there was a close correlation between being old and being poor) closer analysis reveals that this is not necessarily so. In principle there is in fact nothing special about pensions, that is, nothing about them which necessitates state involvement on either (economic) efficiency

grounds or ethical grounds (as part of a general moral obligation to relieve avoidable indigence).[18]

(As things stand today, the state does not force people to save for
old age. It taxes them and puts the money into a pyramid scheme.
Forcing them to save for old age, with property rights in the savings,
while still undesirable, would nonetheless be a *big* improvement
over the current system.)

Moreover, "state involvement in pensions [in Britain] has created
massive problems for the future and very little of its activity has
been directed towards the genuine welfare problems of the uninsur-
able and others unable to cope with life in market society."[19] The
same can be said of other societies where forced social security
legislation and similar coercive measures have caused major disruptions in people's lives, distorted incentives for prudence and care
about one's future, and produced a form of demoralization by weak-
ening the link between one's judgment and behavior and the conditions of one's life and the lives of those for whose care one is
responsible.[20]

We will see, in the next chapter, that even the more sophisticated
efforts to deny people their right to choose, including their right to
choose when, toward whom, and with what assets of theirs to be
generous, do not succeed. The best system of community life is
actually one in which free choice is fully protected, including the
choice to be benevolent toward one's fellows.

5. Blocked Exchanges

Welfare-Statist Vows

A very powerful impetus for establishing and maintaining the welfare state is the view that government ought to "encourage" generosity, compassion, and other benevolent virtues on the part of the citizenry. This is encouragement in name only; in reality we are talking about mandating, enforcing via law and public policy, behavior that is supposed to help others.

Nearly every measure of the welfare state arises in response to lamentations about how it is ungenerous or lacking in compassion to refuse to force redistribution of wealth. That was made very clear in a criticism of laissez-faire capitalism by perhaps the most influential proponent of the modern welfare state. John Maynard Keynes characterized the capitalist system as follows.

> There must be no mercy or protection for those who embark their capital or their labor in the wrong direction. It is a method of bringing the most successful profit-makers to the top by a ruthless struggle for survival, which selects the most efficient. It does not count the cost of struggle, but looks only to the benefits of the final result which are assumed to be lasting and permanent, once it has been attained. The object of life being to crop the leaves off the branches up to the greatest possible height, the likeliest way of achieving this end is to leave the giraffes with the longest necks to starve out those whose necks are shorter.[1]

It is very important to notice that even if that were an accurate characterization of laissez-faire capitalism—which it is not—nothing that Keynes calls for requires the welfare state. What would be needed would be generosity, compassion, charity, and various institutional expressions of those virtues within civil society.

However, the moral case for the welfare state begins with this caricature of capitalist society and then moves to a call for something very different from ordinary benevolence toward those who experience life's misfortunes in greater measure than others. It demands *coercive* measures: government redistribution of wealth (which means confiscation), government regulation of business (which means the regimentation of people's voluntary commercial endeavors), and prohibition (which means forbidding trade in various goods and services).

A clear statement of that is found in Jeremy Waldron's defense of welfare statism. He states that

> charitable giving is morally right, that everyone ought to give something to those worse off than themselves, and that those who would be the targets of coercion in a welfare state—those who would withhold charity—are morally wrong.[2]

Even assuming Waldron is right about what we all ought to give to those who are worse off than we are, "those who would withhold charity" are not morally wrong *in resisting the coercion perpetrated against them.* That resistance could be directed not against providing help but against being forced to do so, which is demeaning to any adult human being. It is a case of a petty tyranny.[3]

The last measure—prohibition of certain kinds of exchanges— deserves further consideration, for it will shed additional light on the nature of generosity in civil society.

To Foster "Generosity"

Some public policy analysts, political theorists, and philosophers believe that if we wish to encourage generosity, we should ban exchanges in those goods and services where such generosity is desired. In contrast, I have argued that the virtue of generosity can be practiced (as well as neglected) only in a political system that fully protects the right to negative liberty, including the right to earn, hold, and distribute private property as one judges proper. I wish to show that blocking exchanges, as the idea of banning trade in certain goods and services is called, would undermine the full exercise of the virtue of generosity.

Virtue may be practiced even under oppressive circumstances. Most political dissidents in the gulags and inmates in concentration camps certainly had the capacity as well as some opportunity to be virtuous (or vicious). The range of their opportunities was, however, severely limited by those who unjustly incarcerated them.

One's "moral space," to use Robert Nozick's term, will be limited to the degree that one's negative rights are violated. If an innocent citizen is forcibly prevented from speaking for 20 hours every day, he can speak honestly or dishonestly only during the 4 hours left. That clearly limits such an individual's moral options. It curtails the person's sovereignty. Others, not the agent, will decide whether and how he will behave. This is morally objectionable. It deprives the person who is the target of such constraints of the ability to take charge of his conduct, to direct himself in life, and thus robs the person of the opportunity to earn moral credit, to become morally better or worse. The agent is unjustly subjugated to the will of others.

One objection comes from those who advocate blocked exchanges. They propose that there are some goods and services that human beings should not sell, and therefore should be prevented from selling, to one another. Furthermore, they say, banning such sales will enhance people's "freedom to choose" to be generous.

The term "blocked exchanges" was coined by Michael Walzer.[4] The central point advanced is that when it comes to activities such as blood or organ transfers, surrogate mothering, and artificial insemination, people with the capacity to offer or receive the good or service involved should never do so via trade.[5] From that it is concluded that governments ought to prohibit any trade in such goods and services. Prohibiting such trade is believed to encourage charitable donations.

If that line of reasoning succeeds, the agents who might engage in such activities will have the choice of either not providing the good or service in question or donating it. The alternative of selling or perhaps bartering it will have been foreclosed.[6] It is alleged that this helps us all become more generous about donating blood. Evidently, the temptation to sell blood is so great for ordinary folks that if they can do it, they will stop donating it even in emergencies.

What can be said about this? To lay it out briefly, first, it is arguably going to provide those agents with no chance of, for example, doing the wrong thing or practicing some virtue other than generosity, such as prudence, with regard to those goods and services. They will, in short, have various opportunities for exercising their moral agency restricted. Second, it will prohibit what may well be, contrary to the assumptions made by blocked-exchange advocates, morally decent trade in blood, organs, and so forth.

In the following pages, I will argue that blocking exchanges both limits the moral worth of generous conduct and prohibits outright some conduct that is often morally worthwhile. I will also suggest some reasons why the idea of blocking such exchanges may appear to be so clearly right to those who propose it.

Goods and Services Not for Sale

Walzer's list includes things that not only should not but *cannot* be sold—for example, human beings (it is not a *sale* but *kidnapping* or *abduction* when they are taken against their will); criminal justice (the legal system, including criminal justice, is *the framework* for exchange and cannot itself be made the subject of exchange); and numerous rights (the rights to property, free speech, freedom of religion, and so on, which are the moral-political basis of the institution of exchange and cannot themselves be exchanged). Talking about buying such things is entirely misleading. "Buying" justice is, in fact, bribery or extortion, not bona fide trade.

Not everything involving the human transfer of values counts as trade; theft, kidnapping, and extortion, for example, procure certain values for people without amounting to trade—that is, the voluntary exchange of alienable goods and services that rightfully belong to the parties making the exchange. Using such terms as "buying" or "business" or "contracting" in such cases involves, at best, irony, parody, or, often, outright cynicism. It is symptomatic of debates about novel possibilities that impatient folks want to win the argument by way of what I dub "premature characterization." Unalienable things such as one's love, status, and skills are not for sale. One cannot sell, for example, one's academic degree, age, parentage, or heritage. We speak of "my citizenship" or "my degree," but only in the sense in which we speak of "my age" or "my weight," without implying alienable possession.

I will examine this topic by considering the position of Richard Titmuss[7] on selling versus donating blood. Titmuss was concerned with the adverse impact of selling on donation. He asked "whether the blood transfusion services and the use and distribution of human blood should be treated as a market consumption good." He believed that if the answer is in the affirmative, "hospitals, nursing homes, clinical laboratories, schools, universities and even, perhaps, churches would no longer be protected by laws or common conventions of 'charitable' immunity; they would be exposed to the forces of economic calculation and to the laws of the marketplace."[8]

Titmuss's point is quite simple: selling blood undermines a decent society because it is an untoward, morally irrelevant, or even odious exchange, one that diverts us from our duty to help. To be "exposed to the forces of economic calculation and to the laws of the marketplace" appears to be without moral merit, naturally, since one is then being pushed around, forced to do things instead of acting from moral deliberation. Or one is indulging the morally odious temptation to reap profits. Both stand in the way of doing what is morally decent, in this case donating blood to those who need it.

That line of reasoning clearly suggests that only *donations* of blood are *morally* proper, whereas selling involves the amoral or, possibly, immoral practice of economic calculation. To promote morality, then, such trade ought to be banned. As Titmuss put it, "Modern societies require more rather than less freedom of choice for the expression of altruism in the daily life of all social groups."[9] So blocking blood trade will increase the freedom of choice to do what is morally right by limiting the freedom of choice to do what is morally objectionable.

No Utilitarian Solutions

Let me mention, briefly, that the position of Titmuss is attacked by some economists, including Kenneth J. Arrow,[10] and, by implication, Elisabeth M. Landes and Richard A. Posner,[11] mainly on utilitarian grounds. Leon R. Kass,[12] who is a medical ethicist arguing from a broadly utilitarian framework, argues that activities such as selling organs should be permitted because they will promote value. His point is not that it is often morally appropriate or that individuals have a basic right to engage in that kind of sale. He argues that there is evidence that prohibiting the sale of blood (and, by implication, other emergency goods and services) harms society—that is, there is an overall loss of provisions in cases of emergencies.

Those approaches are, I believe, flawed. For one thing, they go to the other extreme by reducing too many human relationships to economics or commerce, thus supporting Titmuss's concerns. The neoclassical economic approach to human behavior is well delineated by Nobel laureate Gary Becker.[13] Its basic theme may be put bluntly as, we are all *utility maximizers*, regardless of what is at stake. As the late George Stigler put it, "Man is eternally a utility-maximizer—in his home, in his office (be it public or private), in his church, in his scientific work—in short, everywhere."[14]

One aspect of this thesis is that not only is there nothing morally objectionable about selling blood, kidneys, or whatever, but even when one donates such things, one is, necessarily, just seeking a sort of in-kind benefit from such conduct since, after all, one is *always* a utility maximizer. I write "in-kind" because one is just giving up one quantity of utility in order to get a larger quantity in return. And although "in-kind" benefits are usually substitutes that are close approximations of the good or service being traded, they can be simply something the trader prefers to gain through trade. In that case, feeling good about what one has done is seen as getting value in return for value. But that view, as I argue elsewhere, is either just wrong or an empty tautology.[15] Suffice it to say here that to claim that one does all of the things one does so as to make oneself feel good is probably wrong. People often do things to make *others* feel good—to achieve some purpose that has nothing to do with how the actor will feel—or act out of conviction or principle. It misses the complexity of human motivation to collapse all of the possible reasons for acting into wanting to feel good or maximizing one's utility. On the other hand, the thesis is tautological if the only way one knows whether someone is doing something so as to feel good is by noting that he or she is indeed doing it. In that case, saying that wanting to obtain good feelings from what one does explains nothing. That is because most economists hold that only revealed preferences or utilities can be useful in a scientific analysis and explanation of human behavior. Their reference to the good feelings people obtain from doing what they do amounts to a reference to the very things the people in fact do. So for them to say, "A did act B because A wanted to obtain good feelings from act B," amounts to no more than saying, "A did act B because A did act B."

Furthermore, ethical utilitarianism in general reveals serious shortcomings when compared with virtue-oriented ethics. The value theory undergirding utilitarianism leaves out of account important features of virtue or right conduct. The reason is that, when it comes to considering moral character and conduct, assessment of aggregate results, the central concern of utilitarianism, is not enough.[16] That is probably why, in some ordinary discussions, we often respond with sympathetic understanding to statements such as, "But he didn't mean to do it" or "She did, after all, mean well." We are often concerned with whether some act exhibits moral worth in and of itself. For utilitarians, what counts are aggregate consequences that are difficult if not impossible to predict as one makes decisions. (That may explain why many people make use of utilitarian analysis for public policy purposes but do not apply it so much to discussions of individual moral behavior.)

As Titmuss himself notes, "Givers are in no position themselves to evaluate gains and losses to themselves or to others. Professional arbiters decide but they, in turn, can seldom estimate as individuals the gains and losses for either the givers or the recipients."[17] In matters of conduct, it seems to be more germane to establish whether what we are doing is right *as a matter of the quality of the private action itself, even if consequences may be unknown.* This point is made more clear when we note that in a complex society not all of the consequences can ever be known, so it is impossible for moral agents to undertake such a utilitarian calculus. Even at the political level, when we are concerned with justice, considerations other than the consequences of conduct and policy are important.

Does Justice Require Altruism?

Justice, at least in most cases, pertains to how *individuals* are treated by other people, whether as private persons or legally empowered authorities. In criminal law, for example, justice is partly a matter of due process—that is, the procedure that is due the accused.

Every individual has a right to demand just treatment; if one is not treated justly, he has the right to rectification of the injustice. However, if some conduct is ethically wrong but not unjust, such as the failure of someone to attain a worthwhile goal, no remedy is due. Those who lack courage or prudence or charity are not acting unjustly; they are acting immorally. Some other examples of lack of virtue would be laziness, sloth, dishonesty, betrayal, rudeness, and stinginess. Strong social disapproval of such practices—maybe because of their general adverse impact on human character and relationships—is what is called for, rather than violent reprisals or coercion.

If, however, certain conduct amounts to an injustice, then it requires remedy, because someone's rights have been violated. Some clear cases are assault, kidnapping, rape, murder, robbery, and extortion. An injustice by one, in other words, takes from another what belongs to the other, and that needs to be remedied or punished for society to remain intact and hospitable to human living and flourishing. The legal systems of societies provide justice when their members are required to honor each other's moral space, the mutual though separate opportunity to morally advance one's life. While this approach contains consequentialist elements, it is far from being utilitarian, since it focuses on individual relations, not on aggregate results.

Should we, then, tolerate the selling of blood? Is it an injustice to either those who might sell it or those who might purchase it?

Now, morally untoward exchanges can involve nearly every sort of thing; for example, selling my book or the dinner I cooked to my own child or wife would be morally perverse. It is not, however, the selling per se that is wrong, as indeed seems to be implied by criticisms of selling blood, but selling when one stands in a *familial* and not a *commercial* relationship to the recipient. The creation of a *cash nexus* for all human relationships will reduce them all to economic exchange and fail to take account of the variety of ways people can in fact relate to each other. But there is no reason to think that normal people cannot keep commerce in its proper place.

What further appears to make selling blood perverse is the thought of selling it to someone who is bleeding profusely, perhaps right in front of the would-be seller. Spontaneous donations in such cases would be the morally right course to take, although even then moral rightness would not amount to a categorical imperative to donate. Some people may not deserve such generosity, such as, for example, a serial killer caught in the act. (It is for reasons of the complexity of moral situations that they are dealt with more appropriately in fiction, as opposed to ethics books that give only the sketchiest of cases for us to ponder.)

Is there reason to think that selling blood per se does anyone an injustice? Doing so may at times show lack of appropriate generosity; however, generosity presupposes one's ownership of whatever one may be generous with, so that good or service clearly does not belong to the recipient. Unless it is established that the prospective beneficiary has a claim upon what the agent might donate, refusing to be generous is not an injustice. In light of this, requiring donations

74

rather than trade is wrong. It limits the exercise of the potential donor's moral agency.

So it seems that if sales of blood are prohibited, all that the people who need blood can ask for is generosity or charity. Yet even that needs to be understood by keeping in mind that there is something confusing about acting generously, or even charitably, *when one is forbidden to act otherwise or restricted in one's alternative ways of using what is, after all, one's own—one's blood, surrogate service, or whatever.*

If one is limited to only the alternatives of either donating or not donating blood or anything else, for that matter, then one will not even have the chance, for example, of resisting the temptation to sell it when that would be wrong to do. Even if all trade in such goods and services were morally odious, that still would not establish that it is right to prohibit it. Only if that trade were *unjust* would placing a legal ban on it be the right thing to do. In general, this is what is objectionable about legislating morality; forcing people to act kindly, generously, honestly, forthrightly, decently, prudently, and the like amounts to depriving people of or restricting their opportunity to choose the right course from among many other alternatives that are not unjust.

What about the agent? Is some injustice being done to agents when they are permitted to sell what it might be generous of them to donate?

That idea, in order to be sound, would imply that members of one's community are duty bound to treat one in a paternalistic fashion, because that is owed to one from them as it is owed to children from their parents. Such conduct is appropriate for parents in view of the fact that they have committed themselves to instilling good habits in their children, as well as providing them with various goods and services, when they are dependent minors. Once the children become adults, they need to take over the moral direction of their lives and not be treated as moral invalids.

It seems, then, that neither the seller nor the buyer of blood—or, by extrapolation, buyers or sellers of similar goods or services—is treated unjustly, even if such trade is itself morally objectionable. Still, if it were at best amoral to sell one's blood, and at worst sometimes immoral, the case for blocking its exchange might at least be plausible.

But Is It Morally Wrong?

Earlier I was concerned only with whether it is unjust to fail to donate and whether laws might have to be enacted to encourage donations for justice's sake. What about the point, however, that such trade ought not to be entered into in the first place? Here I focus on whether selling rather than donating is necessarily immoral, never mind unjust.

To put the matter differently, might it be the case that certain goods and services ought to be provided by generosity only, not for any other consideration? Thus, if blood or a kidney or some bone marrow were to be transferred from one person to another, would the only morally proper motivation be generosity and not, for example, a desire for monetary income (a species of prudence in many instances)?

I see no reason to think that this is the case. There is, arguably, nothing at all morally wrong with selling blood to strangers. The contrary view assumes that there is something wicked about intentionally benefiting from providing something to others who need it badly and with whom one is not intimately related. That contention is highly questionable and cannot simply be left as a moral given.

Why should economically benefiting the agent, as well as the recipient, through such actions count for nothing from the moral point of view? The case for the clear moral superiority of donating things like blood (versus selling them) assumes that benefiting others is morally better than economically benefiting oneself, better than seeking to prosper. We do not normally apply such reasoning to food production; we all need food to live, but few people would insist that farmers always donate food, *never* sell it. It is often contended, for example, by Kant, that seeking benefits for oneself counts for nothing *morally*, unless it, in addition, conforms to a moral maxim, although Kant does maintain that we all do benefit ourselves as a matter of natural necessity.[18] He says that it is an indirect—not a primary—duty to seek one's happiness and adds that "all men have already of themselves the strongest and deepest inclination towards happiness, because precisely in this Idea of happiness all inclinations are combined into a sum total."[19]

In other words, many thinkers, including the very influential Kant, believe that self-interest is at most something we follow because we have to, because it is instinctual or unavoidable, but it is only when we do what is in the public interest or abide by some impartial moral principles that we earn genuine moral credit for our deeds.

But if those others to whom one is supposed to be donating count for something morally, and if one is, in many important respects, just like they are, this differentiation of moral standing is unfounded. It certainly seems odd that it is immoral for any of us to benefit ourselves but moral to benefit anyone other than ourselves. It recalls a truly paradoxical line in one of Graham Greene's novels, "None of us has a right to forget anyone. Except ourselves."[20]

Misguided Moral Paradigms and Intuitions

In 1975 John Rawls presented his presidential address, "The Independence of Moral Theory,"[21] at a meeting of the American Philosophical Association. In it he proposed to divorce moral theorizing from the rest of philosophy and argued "that the question as to the existence of objective moral truths seems to depend on the kind and extent of the agreement that would obtain among rational persons who have achieved, or sufficiently approached, wide reflective equilibrium."[22] This amounts to sharing a set of coherent intuitions. As he said, "A central part of moral philosophy is what I have called moral theory: it consists in the comparative study of moral conceptions, which is, in large part, independent."[23]

Intuitions, however, are too loose to serve as the basis of moral judgment. As the following illustrates, they change from epoch to epoch.

> To us today the revelation of the legal murders and cruelties connected with the trial of children are revolting. We have become so habituated to the kindly and even anxious atmosphere of the Children's Courts, that it is hard to believe that the full ceremonial, the dread ordeal, of the Assize Courts could have been brought into use against little children of seven years and upwards—judges uttering their cruel legal platitudes; the chaplain sitting by assenting; the Sheriff in his impressive uniform; ladies coming to the Court to be entertained by such a sight—the spectacle of a terrified little child about to receive the death sentence which the verdict of 12 men, probably fathers of families themselves, had given the judge power to pass.[24]

If intuitionism were right, we would pretty much have to give up on a crucial feature of moral principles, namely, their role in guiding us throughout our lives. For intuitions tend to be temporary, continuously changing, depending on what sentiments happen to be in vogue. Certainly retrospective moral criticism—for example, of slavery, child abuse, patriarchy, political oppression, and racial and sexual segregation—would be impossible, so long as those practices did not conflict with past intuitions. A metaethics that leads to such a result is evidently unsound.

Intuitive moral analysis became very influential following the publication of John Rawls's 1971 book on justice[25] and his abovementioned paper. Until that time, the prominent metaethical position had been emotivism—the view that all moral assertions merely express what the speaker feels about something, pro or con. Intuitionist metaethics sanctions using one's "considered moral judgments," or intuitions that have been examined for coherence and reconciled when coherence was lacking, to address moral questions. Among the prominent factors that shape intuitions, particularly those of moral philosophers, are some of the most impressive substantive moral views that have been handed down through history, as well as one's own particular upbringing. On both counts, there has been a good deal of teaching that denigrates trade and supposes that only charity or sharing has moral merit.[26]

It is not surprising that those who contend that donation, but not trade, has moral value are intuitively predisposed toward deontological or altruistic ethics, or both; that is, many critics of the right to freely trade blood would likely entertain the considered moral judgment that morally decent conduct in general must not have as its purpose personal benefit. For them, the only kind of conduct that is morally praiseworthy is conduct that is helpful to others, especially those in dire need of help. The reputation of Mother Teresa, widely taken to have been the quintessential exemplary moral agent, testifies to both of those predispositions, as does much of post-Kantian contemporary moral theory. Personal flourishing or advancement does not count as a morally praiseworthy motive because it is merely something natural, not requiring a choice and the will to exercise it.[27]

A feature of this ethical legacy and influence on moral thinking is that in order to act morally right—to be morally good as one acts—one cannot be primarily concerned with how one hopes to benefit from the deed. Profit itself cannot be a moral reason for doing something.

Why? Because the moral intuitions of many theorists, influenced by a powerful moral legacy that dismisses prudence, in the narrow sense of seeking to advance or take care of oneself, as of no moral significance, would have it so.

The exclusive role accorded by Kant to the "pure rational" will in determining what counts as moral conduct denies all moral significance to the attainment of goals or ends. The normal feeling of accomplishment one experiences as a result of raising one's own children well, doing one's job well, or even helping another person in need is, according to this view, entirely empty of moral significance if it does not conform to a certain criterion of reason. That seems hardly plausible. Titmuss, Walzer, and others who find donations morally superior to trade assume a moral worldview that, at the end of the day, is very likely to be wrong and that certainly does not correspond to the experiences of (at least) most people.

Why the Concern with Broad Trends?

It may be objected that in this discussion such broad considerations of historical pedigree are irrelevant. However, if there is significance to the work of moral philosophers, surely part of it is that they influence how contemporary and subsequent thinkers view moral issues. It might be noted, in this connection, how confidently Titmuss states that what is needed is "freedom of choice for the expression of altruism," indicating that he takes as given that it is indeed altruism that is the right moral stance for us to take and that there is no room for debate about that.

Thus, although in the late 20th century—when piecemeal moral analysis is the vogue—systematic moral analysis may seem to be out of fashion, the approach of Titmuss and others to ethics is open to serious criticism. The evidence that "the moral point of view," spelled out by Kurt Baier in a book by the same title, is usually assumed to be altruism is hard to deny. Baier, who pretty much set the tone of preintuitionist substantive moral analysis, held that "morality is designed to apply in ... cases ... where interests conflict."[28] This means that morality adjudicates among people but does not guide individuals to the course they ought to take outside of such conflicts.

Therefore, only when one faces the option of acting against one's interest and in favor of another's, as in the case of deciding whether to donate blood, is one involved in a *moral* decision. And, as Titmuss makes quite clear, "the freedom of choice for the expression of altruism"—that is, generosity or charity—deserves to be increased, thus reducing the freedom of choice about one's own happiness or well-being. What other reason could there be for this than that Titmuss and many others take it as given that altruism is the defining characteristic of moral conduct, even though they do not so argue?

The possibility that morality could well involve pursuing one's own successful life—that it may also pertain to choices among alternative goals the agent could pursue, some of which pertain to one's own well-being—is simply excluded in this approach. If self-regarding action cannot be moral because there are already natural inclinations to self-advancement, then overcoming alcoholism or drug dependency could be a moral act only if one were to do it for other people rather than for oneself. Surely one moral reason for overcoming the temptation to drink heavily would be to be a better parent or spouse, for example, but it is contrary to experience and common sense to assert that only such reasons make such an advancement a moral achievement. Surely overcoming ruinous dependence on alcohol or drugs is a moral accomplishment for the childless single person who does it just for himself. To exclude self-regarding actions from the realm of the moral is to trivialize the achievement of those who struggle to achieve lives of dignity and reason.

It is not hard to imagine cases in which selling rather than donating blood could be the ethical, prudent thing to do. In other words, it could easily turn out that after one has paid close attention to the alternatives, in a given situation the most sensible thing for one to do could be to sell one's blood. A college student struggling to pay tuition and bills, for example, might act morally by selling blood occasionally to be able to buy books, to further his education. While generosity is one of the virtues we ought to cultivate and practice, it is not the only one. Industry, thrift, and foresight are also rational for us to cultivate as traits of character and policies for living our lives. In any case, whatever moral virtue is right for us at any given time, in any given situation, the exercise of that virtue must be up to us, not for others to mandate from us by legal force.

Let me make a slight but pertinent detour here. Since I have been discussing influential ideas about morality, let me also make note of the Marxist theory of alienation, especially its characterization of trade. For Marx, selling per se exemplifies alienation, an estrangement from one's human nature. Human nature, in turn, is (eventually to be realized as) fundamentally altruistic and social. As Marx put it quite explicitly, "The human essence is the true collectivity of man."[29] While this view has some of the elements of Aristotelian ethics, Marx restricts what counts as truly human to the altruistic aspects of self-development, leaving personal happiness or flourishing out of the picture entirely. (The reason for that has to do with Marx's concept of species-being and his demotion of personal or individual traits and purposes to the status of trivial pursuits or fetishes, not genuine moral tasks.)[30]

Considering Marx's influence on social and political analysis in our time—due, I believe, in large part to his secularization of ancient tribal sentiments—it is not surprising that some philosophers confidently assume, at least in part, Marx's conceptual influences. They do not bother to substantiate the philosophical underpinnings of the Marxian normative framework; they understand their work to rest confidently and comfortably on previous influential work, just as do natural scientists. Of course, moral and political philosophy are different. Intellectual work in these fields does not have the kind of cumulative character that work in the natural sciences seems to.

In Western societies, which also enjoy the influence of classical liberalism, the intellectually influential Marxist paradigm is commonly applied as the critical framework for analyzing various bits and pieces of commercial life. As W. D. Falk notes, "The concept of morality itself bears the accumulated scars of conceptual evolution."[31]

What Is Wrong with the Legacy

It is an error to assume, without careful argument, that benefiting oneself is always immoral or amoral. Surely, there are many cases in which forgoing a personal benefit in order to help others is the right choice, but one could also be acting morally when one sought one's own success in life, when, for example, one tried to secure financial well-being. It is arguable that all trade has the potential to enhance the life of the agents involved. This includes trade of things like blood. It may, then, be sensible and industrious to secure some benefits via trade; it may be the ethical thing to do. It is ethical, on the whole, to engage in conduct that helps to make one's life a good one.[32]

In short, economic advancement is one facet of a morally good human life. Trade, therefore, can be moral and often is. Donations, in turn, can at times be irresponsible, a kind of generosity to a fault.

Ethics and Free Exchange

Ordinarily we do not rank the various moral virtues we know we ought to cultivate and practice. Which is the cardinal or first virtue: generosity, courage, prudence, or some other? To answer, one needs a moral theory, a conception of the good human life with the needed priorities laid out so that moral problems may be handled successfully.

As I noted above, the virtue that guides us in cases of apparent conflict of virtue or in the exercise of virtues is called prudence, or *phronesis* in Greek. It may be that today this virtue is more accurately captured by the term "integrity," although the language of virtue tends to be somewhat muddled because the subject is so controversial, so many points of view are vying to succeed at getting things right. The prudent person, or one with integrity or discernment, knows how to deploy the virtues and how to balance them to form a good human life. Courage, for example, is not the virtue of always fighting but of knowing when to stand up for what is right (e.g., defending oneself or another person from muggers) and knowing when to avoid an avoidable fight (e.g., by not walking down a dark alley where one might be attacked). The prudent person also knows when to donate blood and when or if to sell it; it might be right to sell it to finance the purchase of college text books but wrong to sell it to a needy relative or friend. Simply blocking the exchange legally does not enhance the individual's moral possibilities; it diminishes them.

It does not follow from the fact that odious or immoral actions are made possible by certain institutions (e.g., the protection of the right to privacy or religious liberty) that those institutions are unjustified. How, indeed, could one choose to do something morally right if all morally wrong things were legally forbidden? The very possibility of moral achievement would be seriously restricted in a society in which immoral conduct was banned.[33] In addition, much of the banned human conduct may not be immoral at all.

None of what Titmuss and others have argued supports the claim that it is never morally right to sell blood. There can be morally justifiable reasons for such a deed. If one has lost one's job, selling one's blood or kidney, or contracting to be a paid surrogate mother, could be one way to obtain some extra funds—perhaps so as to help oneself, one's loved ones, or one's chosen charities to flourish. There is, in short, no reason why one ought never sell one's blood or kidney or bone marrow.

Blocked Exchanges Impede Morality

The idea of this chapter is really quite simple. Titmuss, Walzer, and others believe that donating things like blood is morally worthwhile, while selling them is morally worthless, so we should ban such sales. This, they claim, will enhance moral conduct (increase the freedom to choose moral conduct).

I have argued (a) that blocking other moral options decreases the worth of generosity and (b) that since prudence is a virtue and selling one's blood could well be prudent, blocked exchanges decrease freedom to choose virtuous conduct.

Blocked exchanges do not improve the moral situation at all; on the contrary, they decrease opportunities for practicing the virtue of prudence and diminish, indeed, often make impossible, the moral worth of generous behavior.

Epilogue

The development, cultivation, and exercise of the virtue of generosity is part of the effort to succeed and be happy as a human individual; this virtue can flourish best in a community of human beings that respects the individual's rights to life, liberty, and property. In such a community, it is understood that individuals are responsible for their choices and can do the right thing by choice. That means that they can fulfill their responsibilities to act ethically on their own initiative.

Generosity is morally virtuous because we are essentially social beings with the prospect of intimate human relationships enhancing our lives, and because we can ennoble ourselves by supporting others. Yet if generous behavior were not freely chosen, but instead coerced by law, its moral import would vanish; it would amount to regimented conduct, something for which moral credit cannot be due, especially to the regimented. It would cease to be generous.

We have seen that despite the nondeliberative character of acting on the moral virtue of generosity, institutional—planned—generosity is possible. That is how charitable institutions develop.

Generosity flourishes most authentically as a moral virtue, along with others, in a fully free society, one in which individual rights to life, liberty, and property are diligently protected; to think that the welfare state serves people better than free society is illusory.

Unfortunately, not only do many influential commentators and educators deny all this, but some even charge those who defend the idea with lack of compassion. Thus, James P. Sterba has argued that the libertarian "seems reluctant to take the steps required to secure the basic needs of the poor. Why then does he balk at taking any further steps? Could it be that he does not see the oppression of the poor as truly oppressive after all?"[1]

The best answer to that was provided by the French political economist Frederic Bastiat.

> When we oppose subsidies, we are charged with opposing
> the very thing that it was proposed to subsidize and of being

the enemies of all kinds of activity, because we want these activities to be voluntary and to seek their proper reward in themselves. Thus, if we ask that the state not intervene, by taxation, in religious matters, we are atheists. If we ask that the state not intervene, by taxation, in education, then we hate enlightenment. If we say that the state should not give, by taxation, an artificial value to land or to some branch of industry, then we are the enemies of property and of labor. If we think that the state should not subsidize artists, we are barbarians who judge the arts useless.[2]

To this we may add, "If we oppose forced redistribution of wealth, we are against generosity and lack compassion." Bastiat's reply is precisely on target and is eminently quotable here.

I protest with all my power against these inferences. Far from entertaining the absurd thought of abolishing religion, education, property, labor, and the arts, when we ask the state to protect the free development of all these types of human activity without keeping them on the payroll at one another's expense, we believe, on the contrary, that all these vital forces of society should develop harmoniously under the influence of liberty and that none of them should become, as we see has happened today, a source of trouble, abuses, tyranny, and disaster.

Our adversaries believe that an activity that is neither subsidized nor regulated is abolished. We believe the contrary. Their faith is in the legislator, not in mankind. Ours is in mankind, not in the legislator.[3]

It is, furthermore, begging the question to suggest that when one does not believe the poor own the assets of others and must await their generosity (and not obtain what they might provide via the claim to positive rights), one thinks that they are not oppressed.

If I am able to help someone with my skills but choose to do something else I judge to be more important, I am not claiming that the person who needs the help is not suffering from oppression (by, say, the state bureaucracy or restrictions on the enterprises of the poor). My refusal to help does not make the oppressed person owner of what I have. He never had a right to my life and property to start with, did he?

Of course, in a roundabout way, there is something to the charge that defenders of human liberty are not concerned primarily with kindness, compassion, or generosity, but instead with justice, although not in the way Sterba's rhetorical question suggests.

The function of law is not to prescribe moral virtue but to ensure justice. Of course, once justice is ensured, moral virtue can flourish, although because human beings are free agents, that can never be guaranteed.

At the end of the day, it is best for us to count on the voluntary efforts of human beings, from which all genuine human goodness arises, instead of placing our hopes with aggressive force, something that has rarely if ever produced good.

When thinking about politics and public policy, many people tend toward utopianism or perfectionism. While in ethics that attitude can have a place, since on a personal level someone might do the right thing consistently and without exception, such thinking encourages cynicism when it is directed toward the organization of communities.

Aiming for the impossible—demanding guarantees of generous conduct—must lead to political malpractice: once all the decent paths toward that impossible goal have been tried, it still will not have been reached, so less than decent ways will have to be employed. It is clear that the welfare statists' championing of wealth redistribution—rather than of generosity—falls into the category of seeking to achieve the impossible: the utopia of guaranteed perfection. As the saying goes, the perfect is the enemy of the good.

The welfare state expresses a flawed vision of human moral intercourse: paternalism among adults. It is coercive, presumptuous, and insulting, in the end, rather than kind and generous. No doubt, sometimes support for it stems from a deep and anxious wish to help the unfortunate among us. But even noble sentiments and motivations cannot justify what has been done in the name of the welfare state. The moral enervation of the citizenry occasioned by a paternalistic state that takes responsibility for virtue is one of the main problems we face today. No law can guarantee perfect virtue; perfect guarantees are never available. But the law can create the framework within which free and responsible individuals can work together to achieve virtue. Experience has shown that the virtue of generosity flourishes best when individuals are free.

If the people who currently spend so much time defending and attempting to expand the welfare state were to devote similar attention to promoting the virtue of generosity, practicing it in their own lives and promoting it among their neighbors, relatives, coworkers, and friends, we would certainly live in a world that would be both freer and more generous. We cannot absolve ourselves from the moral requirement to be generous in our own lives simply by advocating that the state take the responsibility from us. The abdication of personal responsibility is one of the greatest moral failures of the modern welfare state.

Notes

Preface

1. Thomas Nagel, "Libertarianism without Foundations," in *Reading Nozick*, ed. Jeffrey Paul (Lanham, Md.: Rowman & Littlefield, 1981), p. 200. This was a review essay on Robert Nozick's book, *Anarchy, State, and Utopia* (New York: Basic Books, 1974).

2. See, for example, Charles Taylor, *Philosophy and the Human Sciences* (Cambridge: Cambridge University Press, 1985); Amitai Etzioni, *The Spirit of Community* (New York: Crown, 1993); Robert N. Bellah et al., *Habits of the Heart: Individualism and Commitment in American Life* (New York: Harper & Row, 1985); and Michael J. Sandel, *Democracy's Discontents* (Cambridge, Mass.: Harvard University Press, 1996).

Chapter 1

1. David Schmidtz, "Reasons for Altruism," *Social Philosophy and Policy* 10 (Winter 1993): 56. Schmidtz considers why one might act altruistically, not as a matter of psychology or sociology, but as a matter of having one's own good reasons for so acting. Whereas I am discussing generosity, Schmidtz is concerned with what he refers to as altruistic acts, namely, being charitable, behaving compassionately, and the like. Those kinds of behavior may or may not be altruistic—in the sense of placing the well-being of others before all else.

Altruism is the term Auguste Comte coined to designate an ethical system whereby others are placed at the head of the list of each person's priorities. It is misleading to designate benevolent conduct as altruistic. Doing so begs the question of whether only altruists—those who accept and practice the system of ethics in which being concerned with the well-being of others is one's primary duty in life—can be generous, kind, or compassionate.

2. Throughout this discussion the concept "habit" will have a significant role. Cultivating or being brought up to engage in good conduct leads to performing such conduct habitually, meaning "without calculation or deliberation." That suggests to some that the conduct in question is practically reflexive and lacks any element of volition. Yet such an understanding of habitual conduct is neither faithful to Aristotle, the initiator of this tradition of thinking about virtue, who believed that moral virtues always include a component of choice, nor adequate for understanding habitual human conduct. In the case of a free agent—whose intentions are a necessary component of bona fide action, as distinct from mere behavior—habit is distinct from deliberate conduct, not in that it lacks the element of intentionality, but in that it sustains conduct as an ongoing policy. What is not present in habitual conduct is a strong disinclination to engage in it—it possesses the feature of commitment, so the conduct is volitional; however, it does not require explicit or overt determination on each occasion when it takes place. One may, thus, have a habit of helping those who deserve help that is not in conflict with or suppressed by one's competing motivations

(e.g., fulfilling one's desires for personal pleasure, safety, or gain). Yet the help is not automatic or reflexive. We may view such conduct as requiring a relatively small measure of "conscious push" from the agent, only a mere continuity of commitment, on the order of the mental attitude of "do it as you are used to doing it." That element is what retains the factor of personal responsibility for such habitual conduct, including credit deserved for it or blame for failure to keep it up on certain occasions.

3. I thank my colleague William Davis for pointing this out to me. It is clearly possible to gain credit for making a choice to remain on the right track, a track that one has been steered toward by other than one's own determination. However, what one gains credit for then is the choice and (self-)determination to stay the course that may not originally have been chosen by oneself.

4. Saying that "evils exist by the voluntary sin of the soul to which God gave free choice" is hardly consistent with counseling *forcing* people to be good to one another. St. Augustine, *Contra Fortunatum Manichaeum, Acta seu Disputatio*, chap. 20.

5. Aristotle defends generosity as a good that is both a good for something and a good in itself, just as are other virtues that aim at the good life. An analysis of generosity along similar but finer lines is developed by Lester H. Hunt, "Generosity and the Diversity of the Virtues," in *The Virtues: Contemporary Essays on Moral Character*, ed. R. Kruschwitz and R. C. Roberts (Belmont, Calif.: Wadsworth, 1987). Hunt especially stresses the element of spontaneity in generosity, which I describe here as nondeliberative, noncalculating at the time when the generous conduct is forthcoming. He also ties generosity to the beliefs of the agent, beliefs that form a kind of background base for generous conduct.

Aristotle argues the view I will discuss later, namely, that generosity requires private property.

> It makes an immense difference with respect to pleasure to consider a thing one's own. It is surely not to no purpose that everyone has affection for himself; this is something natural. Selfishness is justly blamed; but this is not having affection for oneself [simply], but rather having more affection than one should—just as in the case of the greedy person; for practically everyone has affection for things of this sort. Moreover, it is a very pleasant thing to help or do favors for friends, guests, or club mates; and this requires that possessions be private. Those who make the city too much of a unity not only forfeit these things; in addition, they manifestly eliminate the tasks of two of the virtues, moderation concerning women (it being a fine thing to abstain through moderation from a woman who belongs to another) and liberality concerning possessions. For it will not be possible to show oneself as liberal or to perform any liberal action, since the task of liberality lies in the use of possessions.

Aristotle, *The Politics*, trans. by Carnes Lord (Chicago: University of Chicago Press, 1984), book 2, chap. 5, p. 61, 1263141–1263b12.

For more on Aristotle's view on the connection between generosity and property, see T. H. Irwin, "Generosity and Property in Aristotle's Politics," *Social Philosophy and Policy* 4 (Spring 1987): 37–54. Aristotle attempts to defend private property on the grounds that it enables one to be generous, whereas I argue more generally for the right to private property on the grounds that it is deontologically indispensabile (i.e., on the grounds of its role as a necessary precondition of moral conduct within human communities). I argue elsewhere that the right to private property is a necessary prerequisite for moral agency. It secures one a sphere of jurisdiction. See Tibor

R. Machan, "Conditions for Rights: Spheres of Authority," *Journal of Human Relations* 19 (1971): 184–87. I argue that to exercise one's rights—to be responsible for what one does as a holder of legal rights—it is necessary to possess a sphere of authority within which one enjoys the options of a rights holder. And I point out that when private-property rights are denied to persons, so that much of what they do occurs on public property, confusion will arise about the exercise of rights. See also Tibor R. Machan, "The Virtue of Freedom in Capitalism," *Journal of Applied Philosophy* 3 (March 1985): 49–58.

For a different approach that leads to similar results, see Robert Nozick, *Anarchy, State, and Utopia* (New York: Basic Books, 1974), where the author defends Lockean (property) rights in part on the grounds that since they secure one's "moral space," they more readily accord with our moral intuitions than more statist principles would. That is different from the present point, namely, that those rights specify for everyone the necessary domain of human action wherein one makes authoritative, unimpeded decisions and so gains the fruits of, or experiences the results of, one's morally good or bad judgments, thus developing one's moral character.

6. Hunt, "Generosity and the Diversity of the Virtues," p. 244. See also Lester R. Hunt, "Generosity," *American Philosophical Quarterly* 12 (1975): 233–44. This view of rationality is in the Aristotelian rather than Cartesian, Hobbesian, and Humean tradition. The underlying ontology admits of natural ends, and once we have identified something as having a given natural end by using our rational faculty, it is deemed irrational to deny the existence of such a rational end. I will not embark on defending that assumption here except to note that the discrediting of it is largely dependent on the truth of a mechanistic conception of the natural world and/or on empiricist epistemology or theory of knowledge, both of which are dubious views. I might add that in biology there is ample use of such a teleological or end-oriented frame of reference, when the development and behavior of living things are discussed in terms of what such things (e.g., organs, limbs, and various other attributes of plants and animals) achieve and how that achievement explains or accounts for their existence. See, for example, James G. Lennox, "Teleology," in *Keywords in Evolutionary Biology*, ed. Evelyn Fox Keller and Elizabeth Lloyd (Cambridge, Mass.: Harvard University Press, 1992), pp. 324–33; James G. Lennox, "Philosophy of Biology" in *Introduction to the Philosophy of Science*, ed. Merrilee Salmon et al. (Englewood Cliffs, N.J.: Prentice Hall, 1992), chap. 7. Section 7.4 of the latter book argues that natural selection presupposes differentially valuable functional consequences of traits, and thus presupposes teleology.

7. A very strong prescription of the duty of charity is championed in Peter Unger, *Living High and Letting Die: Our Illusion of Innocence* (New York: Oxford University Press, 1996). Unger claims, "On pain of living a life that's seriously immoral, a typical well-off person, like you and me, must give away most of her financially valuable assets, and much of her income, directing the funds to lessen efficiently the serious suffering of others" (p. 134). By this view generosity is quite insufficient as an other-directed moral virtue. One is required to sacrifice, not only one's own well-being, but also that of one's loved ones—as well as the welfare of others, by force if need be—so as to contribute to those throughout the world who are less well off than the rest of us (lest one be guilty of harming, even murdering, those persons).

The utilitarian underpinnings of that position are not made explicit, but once detected they call the position into serious question. For some of the problems with

Unger's thesis, see Colin McGinn, "Saint Elsewhere," *New Republic*, October 14, 1996, pp. 54–57.

8. For a view of the nature of benevolence that regards it as self-interested because it satisfies certain needs one has to feel good about helping others, see Adam Smith, *The Theory of Moral Sentiments* (1759; Indianapolis: Liberty Classics, 1976).

9. Evolutionary processes do bring about changes in various living species. It is only human beings who routinely change from generation to generation, and even over the life of a single individual. That is why the phenomenon of the generation gap is common among them.

10. Adam Ferguson, *An Essay on the History of Civil Society*, ed. Fania Oz-Salzberger (1767; Cambridge: Cambridge University Press, 1995), pp. 7, 12–13.

11. See James D. Wallace, *Virtues and Vices* (Ithaca, N.Y.: Cornell University Press, 1978), pp. 136–39.

12. I discuss the difficulties surrounding this matter in my *Capitalism and Individualism: Reframing the Argument for the Free Society* (New York: St. Martin's, 1990).

13. David Hume, *Hume's Ethical Writings*, ed. A. MacIntyre (New York: Collier Books, 1965), p. 50.

14. David Hume, *A Treatise of Human Nature* (1739; New York: Dolphin Books, 1961), p. 536.

15. Hume, *Hume's Ethical Writings*, p. 31.

16. Ibid., p. 134.

17. Ibid., p. 140.

18. Hume, *A Treatise of Human Nature*, p. 538.

19. Hume, *Hume's Ethical Writings*, p. 139.

20. A very insightful discussion of how sentimentalism can distort politics and law is available in Helmut Schoeck, *Envy* (New York: Harcourt, Brace and World, 1966). A very interesting discussion of the nature of envy and the kind of priorities it leads to may be found in Nozick, especially pp. 239–46.

It is worth noting that the explanation of political policies by reference to envy and related emotions or sentiments can never be the end of the story, lest one leave matters pretty much up to sheer luck, happenstance. Unless the basic cause of what human beings do lies in their *free* actions, which are, in turn, guided by their *free* thought, lamenting bad policies or welcoming good ones is all that is left for us. No argument can make a difference since, as the song goes, "Que será será." An emotion is not something that one freely chooses to have at a given time; it is a response. Emotions may be controlled or suppressed or even formed, slowly and painstakingly, but not chosen.

21. See, for example, Roger W. Sperry, *Science and Moral Priority* (New York: Columbia University Press, 1983). It is important to note that the denial of freedom of thought really implies the freezing of all critical debate: unless we are free to think as we choose, what is the point in saying that another ought to think differently or should have reached different conclusions? All it can amount to is a *lament*, as when one wishes it wouldn't rain on one's picnic when it does.

22. Smith, p. 313.

23. Ibid.

24. See, for example, Robert Axelrod, *The Evolution of Cooperation* (New York: Basic Books, 1984); and Matt Ridley, *The Origins of Virtue* (New York: Viking, 1997).

25. Robert P. George, *Making Men Moral* (Oxford: Clarendon Press, 1993), p. 116.

26. Ibid.

27. For more on this, see Tibor R. Machan, "Is There a Right to Be Wrong?" *International Journal of Applied Philosophy* 2 (1985): 105–9.

28. Douglas B. Rasmussen, "Liberty versus Community?" in *Liberty for the Twenty-First Century*, ed. T. R. Machan and D. B. Rasmussen (Lanham, Md.: Rowman & Littlefield, 1995), p. 272.

29. I thank Douglas Rasmussen for the clear statement of this point. A somewhat different but related view of this topic occurs in Renford Bambrough, *Moral Scepticism and Moral Knowledge* (Atlantic Heights, N.J.: Humanities Press, 1979). Bambrough notes, in the context of discussing the possibility of moral knowledge, that "to claim that there is such a thing as knowledge, or knowledge of such and such a kind, is not to claim to possess such knowledge, or to claim the right to impose one's opinion on others or to suppose that the possession of knowledge would confer such a right" (p. 43).

Chapter 2

1. Earlier I made the point that charity is different from generosity because the former is seen as our duty and is taken to involve giving aid to those who need not deserve it at all, simply because they are in need. Organized charities, however, are not in conformity with this traditional meaning of the term. A charitable trust, for example, may have as its beneficiary artists, educators, scientists, as well as orphans, political refugees, and disaster survivors. Here I use this common sense of the term, not its more technical meaning in formal (duty) ethics.

2. Undoubtedly, even in the midst of extreme hardship, human beings can extend themselves, take a moment to think of others with no concern for quid pro quo, and spontaneously give to those who have a greater need, perhaps for just a moment.

3. Adam Smith, *The Theory of Moral Sentiments*, ed. D. D. Raphael and A. L. MacFie (Indianapolis: Liberty Classics, 1982), p. 86.

4. In this monograph I am following the tradition according to which there exists a hierarchy of virtues for human life, with the possibility that one central virtue satisfies the universality requirement of ethics or morality. At least some virtue(s) would be applicable to everyone who is not crucially incapacitated. And it is also quite possible that, by the dictates of the basic virtue(s), it would be ethically wrong to attempt to exercise some other virtue under certain circumstances (e.g., prudence would be more important for a destitute person to practice than generosity).

5. Still, a given friendship may never offer occasion for generosity if a friend manifests no needs at all.

6. John Rawls, *A Theory of Justice* (Cambridge, Mass.: Harvard University Press, 1971), p. 104.

7. An interesting clue to the difference may be found in the fact that generous conduct is something for which gratitude is naturally expressed, whereas conduct that respects rights—not murdering, assaulting, raping, stealing from and kidnapping people—invites no thanks.

8. John Locke uses the term "property" to encompass all of the above: "Lives, Liberties and Estates, which I call by the general name *property*." John Locke, *Two Treatises of Government*, ed. Peter Lasett (Cambridge: Cambridge University Press, 1988), II, p. 350.

9. See Tibor R. Machan, "Moral Myths and Basic Positive Rights," *Tulane Studies in Philosophy* (1985): 35–41.

10. It is no accident that the greatest source of political conflict in our time is the division of entitlements: Who gets the limited resources that are deemed to be public property and thus something to which all of us have a positive right? Should resources go to AIDS research, the arts, education, public housing, environmental protection, scientific research and development, or other things? A framework of negative rights provides a principled guide to what one is entitled to; roughly, what is the result of one's choices and actions that do not encroach on the choices and actions of others. Nearly all public scandals now have to do with unabashed attempts to influence political leaders about who gets the "public wealth." For more on this, see Tibor R. Machan, *Private Rights and Public Illusions* (New Brunswick, N.J.: Transaction Books, 1995).

11. See Tibor R. Machan, *Individuals and Their Rights* (Chicago: Open Court, 1989).

12. For a careful legal study of different conceptions of rights, see John Hasnas, "From Cannibalism to Caesareans: Two Conceptions of Fundamental Rights," *Northwestern University Law Review* 89, no. 3 (Spring 1995): 900–941.

13. The phrase is quoted by Hart in his explanations of Locke's meaning. See H. L. A. Hart, "Are There Any Natural Rights?" in *Human Rights*, ed. A. I. Melden (Belmont, Calif.: Wadsworth, 1970), p. 82. Hart gives no reference to Locke, and although the idea is present in Locke, I have been unable to locate in Locke the exact words Hart quotes.

14. By moral sovereignty I do not mean that one is the source of the truths of morality, only that one must be the source of decisions concerning whether one will do the right or wrong thing. Suppose Joe compels me with a gun to share my house with someone else. Even if that action of sharing is the morally proper one for me to take, I did not make the decision to behave that way. I cannot gain moral credit for my behavior, or be blamed for its absence, since I was deprived of my role as the cause of it. I was deprived of my moral sovereignty.

There is another argument that I have not developed, namely, that property is often deserved by the good deeds of those who have produced it—that is, property can be the result of prudent conduct. Therefore, to eliminate private ownership of property is to sever a proper or even a just connection, namely, between an act that is good and its results. If Jones's act is good and it brings about Jones's possession of X, Jones's possession of X is prima facie good. The institution of private-property rights acknowledges the wrong of taking X from Jones. See Tibor R. Machan, *Capitalism and Individualism* (New York: St. Martin's, 1990), pp. 83–84.

15. David Levine, *Needs, Rights and the Market* (London: Lynne Rienner, 1988), p. 29.

16. This fact was noted about rights throughout the history of political philosophy. William of Ockham identifies natural rights as "the power to conform to right reason, without an agreement or compact." Quoted from *Opus Nonaginta Dierum*, in M. P. Golding, "The Concept of Rights: A Historical Sketch," *Bioethics and Human Rights*, ed. E. B. Bandman (Boston: Little, Brown, 1978), p. 48.

17. The term "belonging" is used by Charles Taylor in his essay attacking liberalism. See "Atomism" in Charles Taylor, *Philosophy and the Human Sciences* (Cambridge: Cambridge University Press, 1985), pp. 188–210.

18. A recent effort in that direction is Richard Double, *The Non-Reality of Free Will* (New York: Oxford University Press, 1991). I have attempted to defend the thesis of free will in *The Pseudo-Science of B. F. Skinner* (New Rochelle, N.Y.: Arlington House,

1974) and *Individuals and Their Rights*. There are many philosophers who seem to entertain conflicting ideas on this topic, as when they deny that human sovereignty is a reality but, nonetheless, urge us to change our minds to conform to their views. See, in this connection, James Jordan, "Determinists' Dilemma," *Review of Metaphysics* 23 (1969): 48–66. See also Tibor R. Machan, "Applied Ethics and Free Will: Some Untoward Results of Independence," *Journal of Applied Philosophy* 10 (1993): 59–72.

19. "Had to be" because if they could and should have avoided such subjugation, then they may still be held responsible for having placed themselves in a position in which generous conduct was foreclosed to them. And by "could have avoided it," I do not mean that they might have done so at considerable expense or with extreme exertion, as when one avoids being mugged by fighting off the mugger. Rather, I mean that the choice not to be subjugated would be a free, uncoerced choice not involving any considerable resistance to another's forcible attempts. (When a person is battered and besieged in various ways and thus succumbs to subjugation, the subjugation is not avoidable.)

20. Auguste Comte, *Cathéchisme positiviste* (1852; reprint, Rio de Janeiro: Temple de l'humanité, 1957).

21. This is one reason, as I have noted before, that it is very probably true that Karl Marx cannot be said to have advanced a moral theory. He conceived of humanity as an "organic whole" or "organic body." See Karl Marx, *Grundrisse*, ed. M. Nicolaus (reprint, New York: Viking, 1978), p. 100, or Karl Marx, *Grundrisse*, ed. D. McLellan (reprint, New York: Harper Torchbooks, 1971), p. 33.

22. Howard W. French, "The Ritual Slaves of Ghana: Young and Female," *New York Times*, January 20, 1997, p. 4. One priest who supports the practice reportedly stated, "To you this may seem like a miscarriage of justice, but the girl will have to atone. It is the spirit, our fetish, who has made things work this way, and only he can explain." What usually happens is that the priest keeps the girl as a sexual servant until she turns middle aged, after which the family has to replace her with a new virgin, on and on until the atonement has been completed. Could communitarian critics of liberal individualism, with their view of inherited obligations, criticize this practice and, if so, how?

Chapter 3

1. It is ironic, in this connection, that Ayn Rand, who emphatically called herself an egoist, turned out to have done the cause of millions of unfree human beings quite a bit of service by her several novels that called attention, in dramatic ways, to how the loss of liberty can ruin lives. It isn't that Rand was wrong to declare herself an egoist; what's wrong is to regard all philosophical egoists as lacking in generosity.

2. The point has been noted in the literature of contemporary welfare-statist political theory. One work focused specifically on the positive rights of workers is Mary Gibson, *Workers' Rights* (Lanham, Md.: Rowman & Littlefield, 1983). For the general moral arguments for welfare rights, see, for example, John Rawls, *A Theory of Justice* (Cambridge, Mass.: Harvard University Press, 1971); Alan Gewirth, *Reason and Morality* (Chicago: University of Chicago Press, 1978); Ronald Dworkin, *Taking Rights Seriously* (Cambridge, Mass.: Harvard University Press, 1977); and James P. Sterba, *How to Make People Just* (Lanham, Md.: Rowman & Littlefield, 1988). In effect, those political theorists attempt to render the virtue of generosity superfluous by instituting

the practice of legally forcing people to help one another. An extensive discussion of welfare rights is provided in Carl Wellman, *Welfare Rights* (Lanham, Md.: Rowman & Littlefield, 1982), and in Henry Shue, *Basic Rights* (Princeton, N.J.: Princeton University Press, 1980).

3. It is acknowledged by some scholars that Karl Marx's idea that the major means of production are collectively owned implies that everyone's labor belongs to the community as a whole, given that labor is the primary means of production according to Marx's theory. See, for example, Robert Heilbroner, *Marxism: For and Against* (New York: W. W. Norton, 1980), pp. 156–57.

Chapter 4

1. I am using the term "obligation" narrowly; it is, however, also used as a synonym for moral responsibility or duty, in which case the correlation does not hold. I may have the moral responsibility to consider my friend's well-being, but it is not the case that my friend has the right to my consideration. Involuntary servitude is not the result of moral responsibilities to other people.

2. For more on this point, see Tibor R. Machan, "Individualism and Classical Liberalism," *Res Publica* 1 (1995): 3–23. See also Erich Fromm, "Selfishness, Self-Love, and Self-Interest," in *Man against Himself* (New York: Henry Holt, 1947), pp. 119–40; and Tibor R. Machan, *Classical Individualism* (London: Routledge, 1999). Fromm, a neo-Marxist, manages to have a clear understanding of what a robust, naturalistic individualism or egoism amounts to. It is irrelevant here that he builds some confused political conclusions on that understanding.

3. Charles Taylor, "Atomism," in *Philosophy and the Human Sciences* (Cambridge: Cambridge University Press, 1985).

4. Ibid., p. 188. St. Augustine, for example, maintained the "principle of belonging." He held that "every part of the community belongs to the whole." St. Augustine, quoted in *Ethical Issues in Death and Dying,* ed. Thomas L. Beauchamp (Englewood Cliffs, N.J.: Prentice-Hall, 1984), p. 103.

5. John Locke, *The Locke Reader,* ed. John W. Yolton (Cambridge: Cambridge University Press, 1977), p. 278.

6. Ibid., p. 279.

7. For this kind of "belonging," we may, paradoxically, turn to Benjamin Rush, one of the signers of the Declaration of Independence, who wrote about the purpose of public education as follows:

> Let our pupil be taught that he does not belong to himself, but that he is public property. Let him be taught to love his family, but let him be taught at the same time that he must forsake and even forget them when the welfare of his country requires it.

Quoted in Joel Spring, *The American School, 1642–1985* (New York: Longman, 1986), p. 34.

8. John Locke, "Of the State of Nature," in *The Locke Reader,* p. 279.

9. Taylor, "What Is Wrong with Negative Liberty," pp. 211–29.

10. Ibid., p. 212 ff.

11. See, for example, Brian Tierney, "Origins of Natural Rights Language: Text and Contexts, 1150–1250," *History of Political Thought* 10 (Winter 1989): 615–46; Brian Tierney, "Conciliarism, Corporatism, and Individualism: The Doctrine of Individual Rights in Gerson," *Christianesimo hella Storia* 9 (1988): 81–111; and Cary J. Nederman,

"Property and Protest: Political Theory and Subjective Rights in Fourteenth-Century England," *Review of Politics* 58 (Spring 1996): 323–44. See also Fred D. Miller Jr., *Nature, Justice, and Rights in Aristotle's "Politics"* (Oxford: Clarendon, 1995). There is little doubt that before any talk of atomistic individualism, individual rights had been invoked in political discussion.

12. In ancient times the term "justice"—as used in Plato's dialogues, for example— meant something close to what we mean by "perfect virtue." A just person would have been someone who lived a completely ethical life. In later times the term began to be applied mainly to the observance of standards of community life. For more on this, see Hanna F. Pitkin, *Wittgenstein and Justice* (Berkeley: University of California Press, 1970).

13. Taylor allows that there are "certain theories of belonging—which hold that our obligation to obey, or to belong to a particular society, may in certain circumstances be inoperative." Taylor, "Atomism," p. 188. But he discounts that exception and says that "in theories of belonging it is clear that men qua men have an obligation to belong to and sustain society." Ibid. Taylor makes too little of what is, after all, a rather important qualification on so-called theories of belonging. For if a person has the authority to withdraw from a perverse society, he has the authority, also, to determine what criteria to use for that purpose (which may amount to accepting someone else's judgment on the matter). This is not an epistemological carte blanche, of course, but a serious moral responsibility to find out what kind of society is suitable for human flourishing.

14. Consider the following remarks regarding what it means to belong to society.

In a society where everything is nationalised and is the property of the state, anybody can be expropriated and subject to export. The East German Minister of Culture once announced in Leipzig that "Unsere Literatur gehört uns (Our literature belongs to us!). . . ." What he meant was that it didn't belong to you, or to some "common national culture of two separate states" (which the DDR's constitution still mentions), most certainly not to the shared language or the outside world. In Germany the phrase for chattel slaves or indentured servants was *Leibeigenen*, for the bodies belonged to their owners; now we have the new concept of *Geisteigene*, for minds and spirits are also part of the new social property relations. When a bureaucracy considers itself to be the owner of literature, then it has the absolute personal right not only to cultivate its own garden but also to remove ruthlessly such weeds as it deems harmful.

François Bondy, "European Diary, Exist This Way," *Encounter*, April 1981, pp. 42–43.
The concrete reality of such belonging as Taylor finds so appropriate to human social life involves some people's having the legitimated power to decide whether others' ways of living belong or do not belong within society—their religion, recreation, work, literature, or private life. Of course, society never decides any such thing—some other people do.

15. Tatyana Tolstaya, "The Grand Inquisitor," *New Republic*, June 29, 1992, p. 33.

16. Karl Marx, *Grundrisse*, ed. D. McLelland (New York: Harper Torchbooks, 1970), p. 33. Some argue that for Marx this expression served as a mere metaphor, but that isn't borne out by the various texts (e.g., where Marx talks of ancient Greece as "the childhood" of humanity). The belief that Marx wasn't seriously saying such things seems to be influenced by an understanding of Marx advanced by analytical Marxists

such as Jon Elster and John Roemer in the latter part of the 20th century. They find a lot more that is palatable in Marx than do those who take him at his word.

17. Thomas Nagel, "Libertarianism without Foundations," in *Reading Nozick*, ed. Jeffrey Paul (Lanham, Md.: Rowman & Littlefield, 1981), p. 200.

18. Norman Barry, *Welfare* (London: Open University Press, 1990), p. 116. For historical evidence of how countries in which the welfare state is today the norm used, in earlier times, to address the problems that such a state is supposedly aimed at solving, especially the health needs of the public, see David G. Green, *Working-Class Patients and the Medical Establishment: Self-help in Britain from the Mid-Nineteenth Century to 1948* (New York: St. Martin's, 1985). See also David G. Green, *Reinventing Civil Society: The Rediscovery of Welfare without Politics* (London: IEA Health and Welfare Unit, 1993); and Arthur Seldon, ed., *Re-Privatising Welfare: After the Lost Century* (London: Institute of Economic Affairs, 1996). Among those who have called attention to the way citizens have dealt with the needs the welfare state is supposed to relieve, see Melchior Palyi, *Compulsory Medical Care and the Welfare State* (Chicago: National Institute of Professional Services, 1949).

19. Barry, p. 117. The remedy, in political-economic terms as well as those pertaining to personal human morality, lies in what Michael Tanner argues in his recent cogent criticism of the welfare policies of the United States, *The End of Welfare: Fighting Poverty in the Civil Society* (Washington: Cato Institute, 1996). Not even the reforms enacted in 1996 served to remedy the ills of the American welfare state. They ended merely "welfare as we know it," not statist welfare measures per se, that is, the authority of government to usurp the way civil society deals with need, poverty, and even personal negligence. A good start on such a project can be gleaned from Richard C. Cornuelle, *Reclaiming the American Dream*, 2d ed. (New Burnswick, N.J.: Transaction Publishers, 1993).

20. For more on this, see Tibor R. Machan, "Justice and the Welfare State," *Personalist* 50 (Summer 1969): 320–34.

Chapter 5

1. John Maynard Keynes, *The End of Laissez-Faire* (London: Hogarth, 1927), p. 40.

2. Jeremy Waldron, "Welfare and the Images of Charity," *Philosophical Quarterly* 36 (1986): 466. Waldron's purpose is, of course, to defend coercing, via taxation, people to act charitably. His point is, first of all, contradicted by an analysis of the nature of virtuous conduct—which requires that such conduct be voluntary through and through. The underlying assumption that most people would fail to be charitable if left free is refuted by a good deal of historical evidence.

For an examination of the not-for-profit institutions that serve charitable functions and are succeeding at this better than any government, see Peter Drucker, *The New Realities* (New York: Harper & Row, 1989).

Furthermore, charitable and philanthropic activities grew considerably during the 1980s, the very years that most defenders of the welfare state pick on for exhibiting human greed in the wake of some relaxing of government regulations and reduced growth of taxation, precisely the kind of coercion Waldron supports. To learn why, see Charles Murray, "Little Platoons," in *Good Order*, ed. Brad Miner (New York: Simon & Schuster, 1995).

3. See Tibor R. Machan, "The Petty Tyranny of Government Regulation," in *Rights and Regulations*, ed. T. R. Machan and M. B. Johnson (San Francisco: Pacific Institute

for Public Policy Research, 1983), pp. 259–88. Consider that a child may deserve scolding for misconduct but that the same child could be dead right in protesting a severe beating that is supposedly administered as discipline. Indeed, often such severe "discipline" obscures the wrong that the child has done by being an even greater wrong. The citizenry spends millions of its wealth resisting government coercion, via attorneys, lobbyists, the underground economy, black markets, and the like, not always because what bureaucrats want citizens to do is itself found to be objectionable, but because the interference is deemed unjust.

4. Michael Walzer, *Spheres of Justice* (Cambridge, Mass.: Harvard University Press, 1990), pp. 100–103. For a very clear exposition of the central ideas involved in this thesis, see Judith Andre, "Blocked Exchanges: A Taxonomy," in *Pluralism, Justice, and Equality,* ed. David Miller and Michael Walzer (London: Oxford University Press, 1995), pp. 171–96. See also Eric Mack, "Dominos and the Fear of Commodification," in *Markets and Justice, Nomos* 31, ed. John Chapman and J. Roland Pennock (New York: New York University Press, 1989); and Mark Nelson, "The Morality of a Market in Transplant Organs," *Public Affairs Quarterly* 5 (1991): 63–79. At this point, I will leave aside different senses of the concept "free" and use it to mean "uncoerced" or "not intruded upon in one's person or estate."

5. For example, in his campaign for the 1992 Democratic presidential nomination, Jerry Brown argued, in the course of many of his speeches, that "health care should not be a commodity, to be sold for profit" and advocated a universal health care system. Hillary Rodham Clinton, too, characterized health care as a basic right.

6. In the United States of America the practice of bartering with blood is often confined to one's being entitled to obtain blood once one has given it. If one is fortunate and never needs blood, the giving goes uncompensated. That could be considered a kind of insurance purchased through barter.

7. See Richard M. Titmuss, *The Gift Relationship* (London and New York: Pantheon, 1971). Compare with Robert Sugden, *Who Cares? An Economic and Ethical Analysis of Private Charity and the Welfare State* (London: Institute of Economic Affairs, 1983), who argues from the point of view of economic efficiency and concern for abundance of services.

8. Richard M. Titmuss, "Who Is My Stranger?" in *Talking about Welfare,* ed. Noel Timms and David Watson (London: Routledge & Kegan Paul, 1976), p. 211.

9. Ibid., p. 221.

10. Kenneth J. Arrow, "Gifts and Exchanges," *Philosophy and Public Affairs* 1 (1972): 343–62.

11. Elisabeth M. Landes and Richard A. Posner, "The Economics of the Baby Shortage," *Journal of Legal Studies* 7 (1978): 323–48.

12. Leon R. Kass, "Organs for Sale? Propriety, Property, and the Price of Progress," *Public Interest* 107 (1992): 65–86.

13. Gary Becker, *The Economic Approach to Human Behavior* (Chicago: University of Chicago Press, 1978).

14. Quoted in Richard McKenzie, *The Limits of Economic Science* (Boston: Kluwer-Nijhoff, 1983), p. 6.

15. Tibor R. Machan, *Capitalism and Individualism: Reframing the Argument for the Free Society* (New York: St. Martin's, 1990).

16. There is a difference between a theory of value, such as utilitarianism, and a theory of morality, such as altruism or egoism. The former champions conduct that produces value independent of the intentions involved, while the latter focuses on

value that is produced from the right motives or intentions. (I do not wish to get embroiled here with the details of the proper characterization of the consequentialism versus deontologism debate, however.) Thus, it is the latter that is more important for those who are interested, not just in producing value, but in cultivating the kind of human life and community that is deeply concerned with morally right conduct itself.

17. Titmuss, "Who Is My Stranger?" p. 215.

18. For a thorough exploration of the Kantian presuppositions of much of contemporary moral philosophy, see Robert L. Campbell and John Chambers Christopher, "Moral Developmental Theory: A Critique of Its Kantian Presuppositions," *Developmental Review* 16 (1996): 1–47.

19. Immanuel Kant, *Groundwork of the Metaphysics of Morals*, trans. H. J. Paton (New York: Harper & Row, 1964), p. 67. Kant adds that "there is one purpose which they not only can have, but which we can assume with certainty that they all do have by a natural necessity—the purpose, namely of happiness" (p. 83). But what happens by necessity (e.g., breathing or the circulation of blood) is not something for which moral credit can be taken.

20. Graham Greene, *Loser Takes All* (Baltimore: Penguin, 1953), p. 51.

21. John Rawls, "The Independence of Moral Theory," in *Proceedings and Addresses of the American Philosophical Association* 47 (1975): 5–22.

22. Ibid., p. 21.

23. Ibid.

24. Ernest W. Pettifer, *Punishments of Former Days* (East Ardsley, England: EP Publishing, 1974), pp. 35–36.

25. John Rawls, *A Theory of Justice* (Cambridge, Mass.: Harvard University Press, 1971).

26. See Tibor R. Machan, *Business Bashing, Why It's Hazardous to Our Health* (forthcoming).

27. For an outstanding discussion of this and related points, see Douglas J. Den Uyl, *The Virtue of Prudence* (New York: Peter Lang, 1991).

28. Kurt Baier, *The Moral Point of View* (Ithaca, N.Y.: Cornell University Press, 1958), p. 190.

29. Karl Marx, "On the Jewish Question," in *Selected Writings*, trans. D. McLellan (London: Oxford University Press, 1977), p. 126.

30. Arguably, Marx may not even have room for morality in his social-political analysis, given the strong deterministic aspects of his explanation of human behavior. For more on this, see Tibor R. Machan, *Marxism: A Bourgeois Critique* (Bradford, England: MCB University Press, 1988); and Tibor R. Machan, *A Primer on Ethics* (Norman: University of Oklahoma Press, 1996).

It bears noting here that Marx, as many others before him, but perhaps most influentially Auguste Comte, advanced the view that what is most important is service to humanity (or, for Comte, to the Grand or Supreme Being that is society). Thus, when a choice needs to be made about whether individual rights or well-being, or the rights or well-being of the larger social whole, is to be served by public policy, the larger social whole takes precedence.

31. W. D. Falk, *Ought, Reasons, and Morality: The Collected Papers of W. D. Falk*, ed. Kurt Baier (Ithaca, N.Y.: Cornell University Press, 1986), p. 231.

32. For a fuller discussion, see David L. Norton, *Personal Destinies: A Philosophy of Ethical Individualism* (Princeton, N.J.: Princeton University Press, 1976).

33. In this connection it needs to be noted that forbidding murder, assault, kidnapping, robbery, and the like does not constitute coercing people to act morally but, rather, protecting them from the invasions of others. The parameters of proper social conduct, namely, the principles of individual rights, are owed respect and may be enforced because they preserve for nonviolent, nonaggressive moral agents a sphere of personal authority, something required so that they may pursue a morally proper life within their communities. In contrast, dictating that people be, or regimenting them to be, prudent, courageous, generous, wise, moderate, tolerant, compassionate, honest, and the like diminishes the possibility for a moral life.

Epilogue

1. James P. Sterba, "Liberty and Welfare," *Ethics* 105 (October 1994): 64–98. Of course, Sterba begs the question when he asserts that the steps he recommends are the ones "required to secure the basic needs of the poor" (p. 90 n. 41). When one considers that the positive right to welfare Sterba advocates comes to nothing less than the legal institution of forcibly taking from people what they have obtained through their own work or voluntary exchange, or both—that is, coercion—it is clear that Sterba claims that certain kinds of theft ought to be legalized. The libertarian disputes that this is sound jurisprudence or public policy. A national policy of subjecting all those who do reasonably well in their lives to involuntary servitude seems the furthest thing from what is required to secure the basic needs of the poor. Perhaps removing the thousands of barriers to self-help, such as licensing laws for professions (800 or so occupations today require government licenses) and restrictions on merchants, would do much more to meet the basic needs of the poor—especially the need to cease being poor—than ever more confiscation and redistribution by welfare bureaucrats.

2. Frederic Bastiat, *Selected Essays on Political Economy*, ed. George B. de Huszar (Irvington-on-Hudson, N.Y.: Foundation for Economic Education, 1964), p. 13.

3. Ibid.

Index

Actions
  benevolent, 32
  motive for generous, 16–17
  from virtuous traits, 14
  See also Conduct
Alienation theory (Marx), 81
Altruism
  choice in expression of (Titmuss),
    79–80
  of Comte, 89 n. 1
  of Marx, 81
  meaning of, x
Aristotle, 90 n. 4
Arrow, Kenneth J., 71
Artificial insemination, 69
Atomism (Taylor), 54–55

Baier, Kurt, 79
Barry, Norman, 65–66
Bastiat, Frederic, 85–86
Becker, Gary, 71
Bellah, Robert, xi
Benevolence, 1, 4
  charity as, 2
  generosity in friendship, 34
  service to public (Hume), 14–17
  in welfare state, 67–68
Blocked exchanges
  argument to prohibit, 69, 82
  defined, 68
  selling opposed to donating blood
    (Titmuss), 70–71
Blood
  moral justification for selling, 83
  selling opposed to donating
    (Titmuss), 70–71
  selling or donating, 12, 69–76, 82–83

Capitalism, 67
Character
  as collection of traits, 2
  generosity flows from, 1
  individual's responsibility for, 32–33

Charity
  Christian (*caritas*), 4–5
  different from generosity, 93 n. 1
  given from sense of duty, 2
  welfare state forced, x
Choice
  to act virtuously, 58
  in context of blocked exchanges,
    69–71, 75
  in expression of altruism (Titmuss),
    79–80
  of human beings, 18
  protection of free, 66
  between selling and donating blood,
    82–83
Collectivism
  conception of individualism, 58
  "the people" concept, 59
Communal system, 50–51
Communitarians
  criticism of libertarians, xi
  position on liberal individualism, 20
Community
  best system of community life, 66
  flourishing of generosity in, 85
  individual sovereignty in, 41–43
  institutionalized generosity in, 47,
    50–52, 60–61
  paternalism of, 75
Compassion, 1, 23
Compossibility, 40
Comte, Auguste, 43
Conduct
  conditions for limits to generous,
    70–73
  generous, 1, 3–6, 10–11, 20, 93 n. 7
  habitual, 89 n. 2
  intentional and deliberate, 6, 89 n. 2
  moral, 34
  morally wrong, 21–22
  regimented, 85
  respecting rights, 93 n. 7
  unjust, 73–74
  virtuous, 42
  See also Actions

103

104

Human beings
  basic rights of, 40
  choices of, 18, 33
  interdependence among, 53–54
  Smith's conception of, 19–20
  sovereignty of moral agents as, x
  as thinking, rational animals, 9–10,
    18
  in understanding of individualism,
    60
Human nature
  defining, 8
  link to generosity, 8–13
  Marx's conception of, 81
  modern conception of, 20
Hume, David, 14–16, 19
Hunt, Lester, 6

Impartiality in government, 62–63
Individualism
  atomistic (Taylor), 53–55
  criticism of, 20, 54, 58
  in ethics of virtue, 53–54
  historicist objection to, 43
  liberal, 20
  in morally virtuous life, 60
  position on self-development, 57
  worst-case scenario, 59
Institutions
  of free community, 47, 50–52, 60–61
  making certain actions possible, 82
  of welfare state, 48–49
Integrity, 14
Intuitions
  factors shaping, 78
  in Rawls's moral theory, 77
  temporary nature of, 78

Justice
  buying, 70
  as cardinal virtue, 25
  ensured by law, 87
  as fairness, 6
  in honoring moral space, 74
  as people's treatment of other
    people, 73

Kant, Immanuel, 36, 76
Kass, Leon R., 71
Keynes, John Maynard, 67
Kindness, 1, 23

Landes, Elizabeth M., 71

Law
  to enforce morality, 21–22
  function of, 87
Laws of nature (Locke), 55–56
Levine, David, 41
Liberty
  indivisibility of human, 40
  right of, xi
Locke, John
  natural rights, 55–56
  on subordination, 56
Love, Christian (*agape*), 4–5

Marx, Karl, 42, 59, 60, 81
Moral agency
  development and exercise of, 34
  in life of human beings, 60
  limiting, 74–75
  right to private property as
    prerequisite for, 90 n. 5
  sphere of, 38
Moral analysis, intuitive, 78
Morality
  conditions for existence of, 41
  of donating blood (Titmuss), 71
  duties of, 6
  Hume's conception of, 16–17
  impeded by blocked exchanges, 83
  legislating, 21–22, 75
  of Locke, 56
  Skinner's conception of, 16
  theory of, 99 n. 17
Moral judgment, 77–78
Moral life, x
Moral space
  justice in honoring, 74
  of Nozick, 69, 90–91 n. 5
Moral theory
  independence of (Rawls), 77
  need for, 82
Moral vice, 3
Moral virtues
  accompanying generosity, 13
  basic, 7
  fairness as, 6–7
  generosity as, ix, 7–8, 14
  as guides, 24
  independence in exercise of, 80
  limits to, 31
  practice of, x, 36
  See also Virtues
Murray, Charles, xi

106

About the Author

Tibor R. Machan, who is on leave from his teaching position in the Department of Philosophy at Auburn University, is currently professor and distinguished fellow at the Leatherby Center for Entrepreneurship and Business Ethics at the School of Business & Economics, Chapman University, Orange, California. He is also a research fellow at the Hoover Institution at Stanford University, an adviser to Freedom Communications, Inc., on public policy issues, and a syndicated columnist.

After being smuggled out of Hungary in 1953, Machan served four years in the U.S. Air Force and earned degrees in philosophy at Claremont McKenna College, New York University, and the University of California at Santa Barbara. He has written several books, among them *The Pseudo-Science of B. F. Skinner* (1974), *Individuals and Their Rights* (1989), and *A Primer on Ethics* (1997). He was visiting professor at the United States Military Academy, West Point, in 1992–93. He has appeared on *Firing Line* and other television programs.

Machan's next book, *Classical Individualism*, will be published by Routledge. Machan has three children and lives in California.

Cato Institute

Founded in 1977, the Cato Institute is a public policy research foundation dedicated to broadening the parameters of policy debate to allow consideration of more options that are consistent with the traditional American principles of limited government, individual liberty, and peace. To that end, the Institute strives to achieve greater involvement of the intelligent, concerned lay public in questions of policy and the proper role of government.

The Institute is named for *Cato's Letters*, libertarian pamphlets that were widely read in the American Colonies in the early 18th century and played a major role in laying the philosophical foundation for the American Revolution.

Despite the achievement of the nation's Founders, today virtually no aspect of life is free from government encroachment. A pervasive intolerance for individual rights is shown by government's arbitrary intrusions into private economic transactions and its disregard for civil liberties.

To counter that trend, the Cato Institute undertakes an extensive publications program that addresses the complete spectrum of policy issues. Books, monographs, and shorter studies are commissioned to examine the federal budget, Social Security, regulation, military spending, international trade, and myriad other issues. Major policy conferences are held throughout the year, from which papers are published thrice yearly in the *Cato Journal*. The Institute also publishes the quarterly magazine *Regulation*.

In order to maintain its independence, the Cato Institute accepts no government funding. Contributions are received from foundations, corporations, and individuals, and other revenue is generated from the sale of publications. The Institute is a nonprofit, tax-exempt, educational foundation under Section 501(c)3 of the Internal Revenue Code.

CATO INSTITUTE
1000 Massachusetts Ave., N.W.
Washington, D.C. 20001